Twayne's United States Authors Series

EDITOR OF THIS VOLUME

Warren French

Indiana University

William Goyen

TUSAS 329

WILLIAM GOYEN

By ROBERT PHILLIPS

TWAYNE PUBLISHERS
A DIVISION OF G. K. HALL & CO., BOSTON

Published in 1979 by Twayne Publishers,
A Division of G. K. Hall & Co.
All Rights Reserved

Printed on permanent durable acid-free paper
and bound in the United
States of America

First Printing

Frontispiece photograph of William Goyen
by Frank Grizzaffi.

Library of Congress Cataloging in Publication Data

Phillips, Robert S
William Goyen.

(Twayne's United States authors series ; TUSAS 329)
Includes bibliographical references and index.
1. Goyen, William—Criticism and interpretation.
PS3513.097Z8   813'.5'4   78-27472
ISBN 0-8057-7269-3

This book of course is for
BILL
and for DORIS and MICHAEL

Contents

About the Author

Robert Phillips is the author of two other critical studies—*Denton Welch* (Twayne) and *The Confessional Poets* (Southern Illinois University Press)—as well as a collection of short stories—*The Land of Lost Content* (Vanguard)—and a collection of poetry—*The Pregnant Man* (Doubleday). In addition, he is editor of three anthologies—*Aspects of Alice; Moonstruck: An Anthology of Lunar Poetry;* and *Last and Lost Poems of Delmore Schwartz* (all published by Vanguard). He is an associate editor of *The Paris Review*, and has written for most of the major literary publications in this country, including *The New Yorker, Partisan Review, The Southern Review, The Saturday Review,* and *The New York Times Book Review*. He received his undergraduate and graduate degrees from Syracuse University, where he subsequently taught. More recently he has taught at The New School for Social Research, and at the Putnam County Arts Center. In 1976 he was awarded a Creative Artists' Public Service Grant from the New York State Council on the Arts.

Preface

This study, the first to trace the development of William Goyen's writing from the earliest work to the present, discusses the books as they have appeared, including the nine poems published as a separate book in limited edition. My book strives for some overall view of Goyen's work and for a sense of his position in modern American literature, of which he has been a part since 1950.

I stress those works which in my view are central to Goyen's meaning and to his development, and which particularly evoke a sympathetic response from me. My discussions of *The Fair Sister* and *A Book of Jesus*, therefore, are more brief than those of the richer, more rewarding books. I have not discussed Goyen's plays. Three of the plays (*The House of Breath; The House of Breath, Black/White,* and *Christy*) derive directly from Goyen's first novel, the plot and meaning of which is amply discussed. Two other plays, *A Possibility of Oil* and *The Diamond Rattler*, are related both in character and in action to the story "Rhody's Path," and to the novel *Come, the Restorer*—both of which are discussed. To explicate the plays remains for another to do.

To my knowledge the opening chapter is the first biographical piece of any length about the author. I have not attempted, in the subsequent critical chapters, to interpret his works from a strict biographical basis. I leave that to readers so inclined, with the warning that to do so would entail proving, among other things, that William Goyen has been, or has been involved with, a tightrope walker, balloonists, aerialists, flagpole sitters, and transvestites. Had Goyen attempted all the roles his protagonists play, his life would make George Plimpton's appear colorless! Being so rich in fantasy, Goyen's writing seems to defeat such biographical criticism.

Rather, as in my two previous critical studies (*Denton Welch* and *The Confessional Poets*), my method has been a close textual reading and, wherever applicable, a Jungian mythic perspective. I must admit that different books by Goyen bring forth different kinds of responses. In each case I havae attempted to relate the books one to another, to answer his fictional Aunt Malley Ganchion's query, "What kin are we all to one another, anyway?"

The book concludes with a complete transcript of an interview that William Goyen granted me in Katonah, New York, in June 1975, shortly after his sixtieth birthday and the publication of the twenty-fifth-anniversary edition of his first novel, *The House of Breath*. This interview originally appeared as part of the *Paris Review*'s Art of Fiction series, and it remains perhaps the best single source for information on the events and ideas behind the works. Reprinting it here as a long postscript invites the reader who has followed this account of Goyen's life and works to become acquainted with the generating spirit behind them.

It has been said that biographers often come to resemble their subjects. From the outset, Goyen's background, childhood, and origins have been similar to my own. His Southwest is not so different from my Eastern Shore, which perhaps helps account for the sympathy I feel for all his writing. Goyen's novels and stories seem to me to portray the small-town and big-family way of life that still existed when I was a child, and which indeed persists in certain areas today if one but looks. Goyen may be surprised to know how closely I identify with his own responses to life. Like all books, this one has been for me partly an act of self-exploration.

But my chief reason for writing this study is my belief that William Goyen's books have, by and large, been underrated in America. (I say "in America" because during that period when Goyen was totally out of print in this country, one could walk into any of the better bookshops in England, France, or Germany and find there three or four of his titles. During the early 1970s, when I lived in Europe, I had extensive discussions of his work with booksellers and professors there who knew and revered his fiction in a manner surpassing his reputation in this country.)

I do not expect everyone to agree with me, or even to share my affection for some of Goyen's most fantastic creations, though plenty of others have in the past. I can only say that I find his works to be undiminished by familiarity. Goyen's wit makes me laugh, and his introspection makes me think. I find his impact increased by time. A good sign is that more of his books become available in this country each year. At the time I began this study, as I said, all were out of print. Now there are paperback editions of *The House of Breath*, the *Selected Writings*, and *A Book of Jesus;* and hardback editions of *Come, the Restorer*, *A Book of Jesus*, the *Collected Stories*, and the twenty-fifth anniversary edition of *The House of*

Preface

Breath. Since the *Collected Stories* contains all of *Ghost and Flesh* and *The Faces of Blood Kindred,* only *In a Farther Country* and *The Fair Sister* remain out of print at this writing. And Black Sparrow Press plans to reprint the former in the near future.

There are not many people I should thank for help in the preparation of this book which, for better or worse, largely has been a personal response to a relatively small body of work. I am, of course, greatly thankful to Mr. Goyen and members of his family for much personal conversation and correspondence. I have also received insights of a critical nature from published and unpublished commentary by Erika Duncan and by Patrice Repusseau, one of Goyen's French translators. I tried not to borrow too heavily from their writings, and to acknowledge their help whenever I did.

ROBERT PHILLIPS

Acknowledgments

Some material in this book is reprinted or adapted from portions of my earlier writings on William Goyen. Especially I wish to thank the editors of *Commonweal, Delta, New York Times Book Review, Paris Review, Southern Review, Southwest Review,* and *Studies in Short Fiction* for permission to make use of essays, reviews, and an interview I published in their pages.

Margaret L. Hartley, editor of *Southwest Review,* is due special thanks not only for her interest in my writings on Goyen, but for her promotion and publication of his stories themselves. Many originally appeared in the pages of her quarterly.

Finally I wish to thank the following publishers for permission to quote from the books listed, and Mr. Goyen for permission to quote from those to which he holds copyright as well as from other material, including letters to me and to other individuals:

Albondocani Press: *Nine Poems by William Goyen.* Copyright 1949, 1976 by William Goyen.

Doubleday & Company: *A Book of Jesus.* Copyright 1973 by William Goyen. *Collected Stories of William Goyen.* Copyright 1975 by William Goyen. *Come, the Restorer.* Copyright 1974 by William Goyen. *The Fair Sister.* Copyright 1963 by William Goyen.

Random House: *In a Farther Country.* Copyright 1955 by William Goyen.

Random House/Bookworks: *The House of Breath.* Copyright 1949, 1950, 1975 by William Goyen. *Selected Writings of William Goyen.* Copyright 1974 by William Goyen.

The photograph of William Goyen which appears as the frontispiece is reproduced with the permission of the photographer, Frank Grizzaffi.

Chronology

1915   (Charles) William Goyen born April 24, in Trinity, Texas, first of three children and one of two sons of Charles Provine (a lumber salesman) and Mary Inez (Trow) Goyen.

1929– Attends public high schools in Houston.
1932

1932– Attends Rice University (then called Rice Institute); studies
1937   English under George Williams (author of *The Blind Bull*).

1937   Receives B.A. from Rice in Literature and Languages (M.A., 1939).

1939– Teaches literature at the University of Houston.
1940

1940– Enlists in U.S. Navy and serves as officer on the aircraft
1945   carrier *Casablanca* in the South Pacific; meets Walter Berns.

1945– Lives in Taos, New Mexico, with Berns; meets Frieda Law-
1947   rence; writes an unfinished and unpublished novella, *The Well*, as well as his Taos poems; builds an adobe house; first story, "A Parable of Perez," accepted for *New Directions* annual by James Laughlin.

1948   Moves to Napa, California; San Francisco; then to Portland, Oregon, where he teaches briefly at Reed College; *Accent* publishes his "Four American Portraits" (part of what would become *The House of Breath*).

1948– *Southwest Review* Literary Fellowship.
1949

1949   To Paris and London; finishes *The House of Breath* in London late in the year; John Lehmann accepts a portion of the novel for U.K. publication in his quarterly; first book, a translation of Albert Cossery's *Les Faneants* (The Lazy Ones), published in United States.

1950   *The House of Breath* published in August; receives the MacMurray Award for the best first novel by a Texan.

1950– Lives in Manhattan, writing stories for a collection; "Her
1952   Breath on the Windowpane" in Martha Foley's *Best American Short Stories of 1950*; meets Joseph Glasco, the painter, at "The Creeks," the estate of painter Alfonso Ossorio in East

Hampton, Long Island, and lives there for a time in a studio.

1952   *Ghost and Flesh,* first collection of stories, published in United States; receives first Guggenheim Fellowship.

1953–   Returns to New Mexico; lives in El Prado; works to adapt
1954   *The House of Breath* for the stage; Maurice Edgar Coindreau's translation of Goyen's first novel wins the French Halperin-Kaminsky Prize.

1954   Stage version of *The House of Breath* produced off-Broadway; Goyen wins second Guggenheim.

1954–   Lives in Rome.
1955

1955   Returns to New York City; *In a Farther Country* published.

1955–   Instructor of the novel, drama, and short story at The New
1960   School for Social Research.

1956   Returns to El Prado in June; *Zamour und andere Erzahlungen,* containing unpublished short stories, published in Frankfurt.

1957   Film version of "The White Rooster"; resumes residence in Manhattan.

1958   Release of *The Left-Handed Gun,* film with song lyrics by Goyen.

1960   New play, *The Diamond Rattler,* produced at Charles Playhouse in Boston; second collection of stories, *The Faces of Blood Kindred,* published.

1961   Television play, *A Possibility of Oil,* produced; "A Tale of Inheritance" in *Best American Short Stories of 1961;* reading tour of Germany.

1962   Remains in Germany.

1963   Returns to America; marries Doris Roberts on November 10; fourth play, *Christy,* produced at American Palace Theatre, with Actress Doris Roberts; third novel, *The Fiar Sister,* published in United States, England, and Germany.

1963–   Receives Ford Foundation Grant for Theater Writing, Lin-
1964   coln Center Repertory Company, New York.

1964   *Short Stories by William Goyen,* including several unpublished, edited by Erwin Helms and published in Germany; "Figure Over the Town" in *Best American Short Stories of 1964.*

1964–   Lecturer in English at Columbia University.
1965

1965   Begins work on book of memoirs, tentatively titled *Six Women*.

1966–   Senior Trade Editor for McGraw-Hill in New York.
1971

1969   Playwright-in-Residence, The Trinity Square Repertory Company; fifth play, a second stage version of *The House of Breath* (titled *The House of Breath, Black/ White*), produced in Providence; presents files of personal correspondence (1940–1963) to Rice University.

1970   In September becomes visiting professor in the Writing Program, Brown University.

1971   July, on staff of Southwest Writers' Conference, Houston; resigns from McGraw-Hill, October 29, to spend full time on writing.

1972   Three weeks' residency at Brown University.

1973   First nonfiction book, *A Book of Jesus*, published; July, at Southwest Writers' Conference and Brown University.

1974   *Come, the Restorer* published; musical play, *Aimee!*, produced by Trinity Square Repertory Company; *Selected Writings of William Goyen*, April; new ballet by Martha Graham, *Holy Jungle* (based upon *The House of Breath*), staged; teaches at Brown all year.

1975   Twenty-fifth anniversary edition of *The House of Breath* published; *Collected Stories of William Goyen;* moves to Los Angeles in June.

1976   *Nine Poems by William Goyen* published in limited edition; "Bridge of Music, River of Sand" selected for O. Henry Awards volume; becomes writer-in-residence, Princeton University, fall semester.

1977   Returns to Princeton to teach; receives Distinguished Alumni Award, Rice University, May; published new stories in *Redbook* and *Ontario Review*.

1978   Terminates teaching at Princeton in June; divides time between New York and Los Angeles; delivers talk, "While You Were Away," at Houston Public Library as part of "Our Urban Past, Present, and Future" series made possible by The National Endowment for the Humanities.

1979   William Goyen issue of *Delta* published by l'Université Paul Valéry at Montpellier.

CHAPTER 1

"What I Wanted Was to Make Splendor"

We become what we sing.—Matthew Arnold

The World exists not merely in itself,
but also as it appears to me.—C. G. Jung

I *Beginnings*

C HARLES William Goyen was born in Trinity, Texas, on April
24, 1915. The town was a thriving railroad and sawmill town by
the Trinity River in East Texas. His father, Charles Provine Goyen,
came from a Mississippi family and was a lumber dealer. His
mother, Mary Inez Goyen, née Trow, was a Texan. Her family was
composed of carpenters, but her father was the town postmaster for
many years.

It was a pastoral Texas landscape into which William was born, a
landscape to be celebrated in all his books. He grew up around a
sawmill, and wood and the love of wood is to be found throughout
his work. His father always came home with sawdust in his pockets
and his shoes.[1] Goyen came to realize in time, as does the protagonist of his story "Old Wildwood," that "he loved wood best and
belonged by his very secret woodsman's nature to old wildwood."[2]

Goyen spent his infancy and childhood in a large old house belonging to his grandmother in Trinity, a house very much like that
depicted in *The House of Breath* and in many of the stories in *The
Faces of Blood Kindred*—a house so full of relatives, some
Methodist, some Catholic, that the boy and later the man is moved
to question, "What kin are we all to each other?"[3] He also had a
brother and a sister.

It seems safe to assume that the young Goyen was every bit as
sensitive as his creation, Boy Ganchion, of that first novel. Far

17

removed from the city, or even a town, his life was the bustle of the household and the animation of the river, the trees, the pasture. Indeed, Goyen later came to describe the landscape as a living thing: ". . . a little patch of woods behind the house that I remember. It had bearded trees that clicked and ticked and cracked and cheeped and twittered."[4] We also recall that, in *The House of Breath,* the river is a central character with a voice all its own. In several of Goyen's tales, he projects himself directly into the minds of snakes and of roosters. In short, his sympathy, even empathy, with nature has been highly developed, perhaps because of his isolation and communication with nature as a child.

We can also assume that, in that house of so many adults, the young Goyen heard many tales told. Indeed, the majority of his stories are narratives, someone telling someone else a tale. Goyen acknowledges this. In the Preface to his *Collected Stories* he writes,

Somebody is telling something to somebody—an event: who's listening? Where's the listener? For me, as I write, the listener is always present. It may be me. Or, of course, the reader. But, for me, I've been mainly interested in the teller-listener situation. I've not been interested in simply reproducing a big section of life off the streets or from the Stock Exchange or Congress. I've cared most about the world in one person's head. Mostly, then, I've cared about the buried song in somebody; or the music in what happened.

And so I have thought of my stories as folksong, as ballad or rhapsody. This led me, naturally, to be concerned with speech, lyric speech—my heritage. Since the people of the region where most of my stories emanate—or hover over (they do, I believe, move in and through the Great World)—are natural talkers and use their speech with gusto and almost operatic delivery; and since the language of their place is rich with phrases and expressions out of the Bible, the Negro imagination, the Mexican fantasy, deep South Evangelism, the jargon of the cottonfield and cotton gin, of the oil field, railroad and sawmill, I, coming up among them, had at my ears a glorious sound, and in my hand a marvelous instrument of language, given to me. I worked at this instrument as though it were a fiddle or a cello, to get the music out of it; and I was finally able to detach myself from this speech so as to be able to hear it almost as a foreign language. . . .[5]

This large family in which Goyen grew up supplied him not only with a love of the Bible and a love of language; they also created his awareness of superstition, a force felt behind much of his work. He also received his first schooling at home, from his uncle, in a situation reminiscent of Christy and Boy in *The House of Breath*: "In the kitchen, tacked on the wall by Christy, was a map of the world."[6] Goyen lived in Trinity until he was seven. Then his immediate family moved, for one year only, to Shreveport, Louisiana. The Goyens then returned to Texas, settling this time in Houston. From the third grade onward, he was educated in that city: grammar school, junior high school, high school, university, even graduate school.

During his younger years, Goyen fished from time to time at Galveston and made trips back to Trinity for family gatherings in that grandmother's house. He was, in all probability, much like "the Cousin" described in the story "The Faces of Blood Kindred"— brown and shy and worried too much about things and afraid of adventure.[7] Goyen has given a direct description of his young self in the Introduction to his *Selected Writings:*

As a child, I was quick and scared; serving, secretly unsettled; imaginative and nervous and sensual. When I reached Sam Houston High School, I thought surely I would be a composer, actor, dancer, singer, fantastico. My mother and father were embarrassed by such ambitions. Nevertheless, I found a way to study dancing, music composition, singing, clandestinely. When this was found out by my parents, who were outraged by the extents of my determination, I did not run away from home to a city. I decided to go underground at home, and write. No one could know that I was doing that. It was my own. This was in my sixteenth year, and what I wrote was lyrical, melancholy, yearning, romantic and sentimental. Above all, it was home-sick—and written at home.[8]

In the opening statement of an interview in the *Paris Review*, he tells how he became a writer of words rather than of music, despite his foremost ambition as a boy to be a composer.[9]

He grew into a tall, lanky, and handsome young man who, in 1932, entered Rice University (then called Rice Institute). When he revisited that university in 1975 to lecture and read from his newest novel, one of the professors there reminded him how he had hated the school at the time. In his Introduction to the *Selected Writings*, Goyen himself called college "intolerable": "I hated the classes, the courses, the students. I wanted to make up new things, not 'study' what had already been made."[10] But in his junior year, the "thunderstrike" (his word) occurred: the young man discovered Shakespeare, Chaucer, Milton, Yeats, Joyce, Flaubert, Turgenev, Balzac,

Melville, Hawthorne, the French Symbolists. . . . Of this period, he writes:

I was at literature, insatiable, for the next three years, reading and writing under the glow and turmoil of what I was reading. Suddenly—it seemed—I had accomplished the Master's Degree in Comparative Literature (1939). I had been writing plays and stories, and in my Junior and Senior years I took all the prizes in both forms.[11]

That master's degree was granted two years after the taking of his undergraduate degree. Goyen taught at the young University of Houston during the 1939–40 academic year.

II   *Vocation*

Then came World War II. Goyen enlisted in the U.S. Navy, and served four and a half years, three and a half of them spent on an aircraft carrier, the *Casablanca,* in the Pacific. Once again the young man was isolated from the real world beyond. Goyen has written very little fiction about his service experiences. Perhaps some of Christy's life as a sailor in the Merchant Marine can be read as Goyen's own. In any event, the war itself was not of importance to Goyen's literary imagination. Rather than aspire to write a great novel out of the war, as Norman Mailer and Irwin Shaw and James Jones and Thomas Heggen all aspired, Goyen once more was homesick and began writing homesick stories—works which did not appear in print until years after the war.

The House of Breath itself was not begun in earnest until Goyen was out of the service, composed furiously between 1945 and 1949. Though not about the war, and not written during the war, Goyen has said of it, "The war had a great deal to do with the writing of the novel. The war necessitated this kind of novel, which I would have written but perhaps much later on. But all of it boiled up in me— this search for a place and an identity." Goyen concludes, "So, I didn't resent the war."[12]

When the war ended, Goyen did not rush into a civilian job, attempting to make up for lost career time. Instead, he chose to travel and to begin his serious writing. This was a very conscious decision. He has written that, during the war, he had determined, if he lived, to return to a basic, simple life of writing.[13] He had decided on someplace near San Francisco, a city which had excited him during the two or three port calls the *Casablanca* made there. So at war's end he returned, briefly, to visit his family in Houston, then set out in an old car from Houston for San Francisco.

He never got farther than New Mexico. Goyen passed first through Sante Fe, then Taos, stopped at Taos, and stayed. At the time, he was not aware that this locale was the home of D. H. Lawrence's widow, Frieda, and the site of a literary community:

It was a landscape I wanted, and needed. I stayed. I knew few people there—as long as I lived there. It was a life-or-death fight to write and to live from what I had to write (not, absolutely not, from what "income" my writing would bring me—for me, then, what had "income" to do with writing? Writing was a Way of Life.)[14]

During these Taos years, roughly 1945–47, Goyen wrote furiously and remarkably. His stories, and sections of the novel, began to appear in *New Directions, Horizon, Accent,* and *Partisan Review.* Parts of the novel, appearing in the literary quarterlies, attracted the eye of the eminent German critic Ernst Robert Curtius. Curtius was in America to lecture at the Goethe Centennial in nearby Aspen, Colorado. Then he motored to El Prado and was the house guest of Helene Wurlitzer. While in El Prado he met Goyen, and a powerful literary friendship began. After *The House of Breath* appeared, Curtius translated it and wrote the preface for the German edition.

Another important friendship built during these years was one with Frieda Lawrence. Goyen was not in the least impressed by the growing legend of D. H. Lawrence, which seemed, he thought, to be perpetuated mainly by the wrong people:

I *loathed* all that—what little I knew of it when I came to New Mexico. What I learned of it after I got to New Mexico, I spat out and turned away from. I simply was *not* "literary," knew nothing of Salons, Writers' Groups, etc.—instinctively I fled all that; was scared and inarticulate, anyway; *never* wanted to be around writers and the sophisticated literary world. Frieda's was my first deep, instinctual, primitive friendship with a woman. We did not talk books or writing. It was a long time before she ever read a word of what I was writing. Our friendship had nothing to do with her writing or my writing—*any* writing. I was seeking the simplest life, a *ground* life; Frieda, despite her life with Lawrence, had always kept to that kind of life. Her life with Lawrence didn't—and still doesn't—interest me. I was never around when worshippers of Lawrence appeared at Frieda's doorstep—I vanished. . . .[15]

That Frieda Lawrence was one of the two people to whom Goyen dedicated his first book is indication enough of the esteem in which he held her friendship. When she died, it was Goyen who helped bury her and read over her grave. She left him the manuscript of one of Lawrence's short stories, and a wall hanging Lawrence had painted. The manuscript he later sold, in a hard time, to Frances Steloff, of the Gotham Book Mart. She gave him $200, which seems very little for an unpublished and signed Lawrence manuscript.

Other close friends of this New Mexico period included Dorothy Brett, another early influence on his life; Mabel Dodge Luhan; Margo Jones; and Walter Berns, another ex-serviceman who helped build and share the little adobe house in which Goyen lived on land gifted him by Frieda. It was to Walter and to Frieda that Goyen dedicated *The House of Breath*.

And what was Goyen's intention in writing that novel? As stated in his own "Note on the Twenty-fifth Anniversary of This Book," he says, ". . . most of all I could hope it would encourage young people to sing out of themselves their own music, to reveal long-kept secrets, to disclose hidden hurt, to make connections with their beginnings, to realize the extent of their relationship to their own at home and to the great mysterious world."[16] Elsewhere Goyen states his intentions and accomplishments during these years in this way:

It was clear to me now: I saw my life as a writing life, a life of giving shape to what happened, of searching for meaning, clarification, entirety. It was my way: expression in words. From then on, I managed to write, with little or no money, with growing distinction—which, I have come to see, brings little usable reward—awards, honors, little money. What I wanted was to make splendor. What I saw, felt, knew was real, was more than what I could make of it. That made a lifetime task, I saw that. All forms of writing excite me and pain me and labor me; but the printed word, the Book—especially the short narrative form—most challenges and most frees me.[17]

After Frieda's death, Goyen left New Mexico, arriving—two years after he set out for it—at San Francisco. If the story "Nests in a Stone Image" (from *Ghost and Flesh*) can be read as autobiographical, Goyen was most unhappy at this time, anxious, tormented, burning. Leaving New Mexico had closed a chapter in his life as surely as leaving Houston had before: "Now he knew that something was all over, that through all the little hotel, in every room, something was finished, and that another long beginning had begun."[18]

From San Francisco he moved to the nearby village of Napa, where—money exhausted—he secured a teaching position for half a year. Goyen's sense of alienation at the time can be inferred from his story "Tenant in the Garden," in which a stranger in the midst of a northwestern community will not be allowed to live his own way. The story is at once a parable of the artist in society and also a projection of Goyen's feelings in Napa. This was the year in which he received the *Southwest Review* Literary Fellowship for work on *The House of Breath,* which was of course still in progress and work on which had slowed due to teaching. Another reason the writing of the novel took nearly five years is that Goyen was continually experimenting, primarily with language, attempting to find the proper way to say what he had to say: "I was trying to find a language I thought I could use for a long time to come. . . . I think young writers really have to find out where they belong, and what their language is."[19]

Goyen has always felt it vital for a writer to find his own speech. In the 1950 interview with Harvey Breit, he declared,

If one is making literature, one is going to make it out of language, out of words, so that he must find that kind of speech that carries more than a line of words. It is not just a question of telling stories, or making poetic statements; like a painter, he must discover what his stuff—which is words—will do. He must discover his authentic speech. Without that there can be no art. As Proust said, Language is more than a style or embellishment, it is a quality of vision. (*New York Times Book Review*)

Which, perhaps, is a simplification of what Goyen was struggling to find in these apprentice years. His own voice, surely. But what of the adequate form and content, once an authentic voice—the authentic voice—is achieved? If we are to look for what is essential in *The House of Breath* and all the books which follow it, we are not likely to find it on the surface of the writing. Goyen's books are not charming pieces of local color or "regional writings" whose purposes are to inform and amuse. No, not so. His intentions from the beginning have been to dive down farther than his fellow writers, and to

stay down longer beneath the consciousness, to explore the
psyche's lower depths in a new way. (These intentions would not
appear to extend to his comic novel, *The Fair Sister*, which seems
primarily to have been written to amuse.) As in any authentic artist,
the "meaning" in Goyen is contained in the total arrangement and
order of his symbols, and, as the critic William Troy observes, "In
the novel everything—people, events, and settings—is capable of
being invested with symbolic value."[20]

Which is to say, William Goyen's works are not superficially
realistic, but subjective, works of flux and intuition which directly
reflect their creator's sensibility. Life for Goyen then, and now,
seems painful less for what it has done to him than for what his
excessive sensitivity causes him to make of it.

Goyen's extensive experiments in the region of language, then,
led him, among other places, to finding a unique shape for his first
novel. As he said in 1950, "It seems to me the novel might very well
have the right to go on establishing its shape in new ways. . . . It's
always seeking its own level, shaped only by itself, not by anything
else. I think prose has the right to be lyrical, to sing. It has the right
to be a miracle, to contain the miraculous."[21]

The novel he produced, of course, not only contains the miraculous, but is in itself a bit of a miracle in its originality. For the
novelist of sensibility, the most embarrassing of all problems has
been that of form, from Richardson through Virginia Woolf to
Goyen himself. The problem is continually one of reconciling im-
measurable experiences of feeling in the measurable form of the
novel. Goyen's pursuit of an adequate form for his subjects was
resolved when he decided upon the novel as a series of self-con-
tained monologues, each reflecting a different character's point of
view.

In *The House of Breath*, the series of monologues are strung
along, one after another, like so many beads, and tied at the back by
the thread of a common family, a common locale, even a common
house for all the characters. Throughout this novel, and the others,
Goyen seems concerned not so much with the relation of events to
character, but their relation to sensibility. This is achieved through
a poetic rendering of his characters' thoughts, dreams, desires, and
fantasies, as well as through the use of rather overt symbols—en-
larged images which are constant and outside the limited experience
of his characters. (The aforementioned map in *The House of Breath*

is one such symbol; the horse as Pegasus in *Come, the Restorer* is another.) What one derives from a Goyen novel, then, is not so much life as a very special vision of a special kind of life—although, as his life work progresses from book to book, we perceive him (especially in the recent *Come, the Restorer*), attempting to maintain a delicate balance between outer and inner realities, between the public and the personal.

Certainly the outer realities of his life as a teacher in Napa were not compatible with his inner world and needs. By now he had a publisher—Random House—for the incomplete novel, on the strength of those portions which had appeared in quarterlies. With this encouragement and a small advance against royalties, Goyen fled for London, but not without taking adverse advice:

When I was two-thirds through my first novel, *The House of Breath*, I announced to my editor, Robert Linscott, that I was going to live in Europe. He was astonished that I would make such a radical move and seriously concerned that the book would lose focus and vitality. I went, and the immense experience disturbed my concentration not at all: what I saw in Europe I put right into my novel: it fit very well—cathedrals, grand avenues, plazas, noble ruins—into the little town of Charity that I was creating out of my own home town of Trinity, Texas.[22]

In London, he met the poet and publisher John Lehmann (later a Commander of the British Empire). Lehmann published in his quarterly magazine yet another section of the novel-in-progress. And finally, late in 1949, the novel was completed in London. *The House of Breath*, published in 1950, received the kind of reviews of which writers dream. To understand the extraordinary reception the book received, one must quote from the reviews themselves, and consider the quality of the minds doing the reviewing:

Stephen Spender called the book a first novel "of astonishing achievement. It is also a further development of what has been the most fruitful discovery of novelists of this century: the invocation of and entry into the innermost existence of each one of a group of several characters. The complex symbolism and imagery develop out of a fundamental simplicity, indicated best by the name of the town which is the center of the lives of the characters—Charity. A profound sympathy with the humblest and poorest men and women combined with a great poetic insight constitute Mr. Goyen's wonderful and rare gift."[23]

In the *New York Times,* Katherine Anne Porter wrote: "There are long passages of the best writing, the fullest and richest and most expressive that I have read in a very long time."[24]

Elizabeth Bowen claimed, "*The House of Breath* impressed, exalted, and moved me. William Goyen has fired his prose into poetry. As a concept, his novel seems to me sane and strong. In our day, humanity needs such a voice as this. America must, surely, acclaim in William Goyen an artist of whom any country would be proud."[25]

And Christopher Isherwood said, "Here is a truly original and arresting voice in our literature. Mr. Goyen is already completely himself, and this first novel is a work of mature art—not merely clever or promising—to be judged seriously on its own terms. Everyone who honestly cares about good writing should read it."[26]

And so the reviews went. Goyen was wined, dined, and celebrated in New York. The novel won the MacMurray Award for the best first novel by a Texan, but was edged out for the very first National Book Award in Fiction by the *Collected Stories* of William Faulkner. The book then was published in England, in the Curtius translation in Germany, and in France. Much later, Maurice Coindreau, eminent critic and translator, wrote to the author, "Do you know that your masterpiece is still considered in Parisan literary circles the best thing that America sent us in this century?"[27]

From such acclaim, one would safely assume that William Goyen had firmly established his reputation within the generation of other American novelists publishing well-received books between the end of the war and 1955—Norman Mailer, Saul Bellow, Truman Capote, William Styron, Vance Bourjaily, Merle Miller, Frederick Buechner, Gore Vidal, Bernard Malamud. Not so. Despite the granting of a Guggenheim Fellowship in 1951, and the publicaton of a truly astonishing book of stories in 1952—*Ghost and Flesh*—Goyen often was dismissed as a regional writer, as one of the "Southern Gothicists." By the time his third book and second novel, *In a Farther Country,* was published in 1955, he felt moved to pen a note for the dust jacket. It read:

I am tired of being called a young Southern writer . . . and am fully forty, from Texas, which is the Southwest, and have had little to do with what has been called "The Southern Literary Revival." Though my father and his family are from Mississippi, I have never lived in that or any other Southern state, only passed through them on a train. The language of my work up to the present novel . . . where it has been regional idioms, has been based on that of Texas, which I know and speak and carry in my ears; it is not Southern. The themes of my work have no affinity with the eccentricities of Southern personality or Gothic bizarreries, though my work has been attracted into that category by spurious association.[28]

These words were written in New York City, far from the South or even the Southwest. Goyen had returned, taking residence in Manhattan after leaving London in 1949. He remained there until 1952 when, armed with a second Guggenheim grant, he returned to New Mexico, to his adobe house near Taos. He had begun *In a Farther Country* in Manhattan, and wished to complete it in Taos, which he did. The book bears the stamp of both places, being about a Southwestern lady who lives in Manhattan but dreams she is in the Southwest, or vice-versa. Goyen remained in Taos for two years, attempting next to adapt *The House of Breath* for the stage. He also began some new short stories, stories which eventually would be gathered in *The Faces of Blood Kindred*. Among his friends in Taos at this time were the poet Arthur Gregor and the art administrator (later turned novelist) Robert Carter. Among his acquaintances in New York was Anais Nin, who describes him at this stage of his life in Volume 6 of her *Diaries*.

The year 1954 found Goyen back in Manhattan, helping stage the dramatic version of *The House of Breath*. The play won an Obie Award for one of the principals, the actress Marguerite H. Lenert, who played Malley Ganchion Starnes (a role she was to repeat in the 1969 Trinity Square Playhouse production as well). The play done, Goyen left for Rome, a city of stone which caused him once more to be homesick for his Texas wildwood. "Rome," he wrote to quarterly editor Margaret L. Hartley, "is a tearing of one's flesh and a deep holy call, the splendid shell of its ruins smell of flesh and grass, so surely the people is grass that the wind bloweth over and withereth; Rome is . . . old, a testament (for me) to what men do with flesh and stone: to lean against the marble of the Caesars is to scald one's flesh and freeze his bone. So much to say . . . I wander, I look, keep my notebooks and write."[29] Here he worked on a novel titled, not surprisingly, *Surely, the People Is Grass*. And more stories were written here, stories which, with the Taos group, became *The Faces of Blood Kindred,* a book which was not published until a full five years later.

After his return from Rome in 1955, until 1960, Goyen again immersed himself in the academic world. This time he was instructor in the novel, drama, and short story at The New School for Social Research in Manhattan. He divided his residence between various Manhattan apartments and an old farmhouse in Ottsville, in Pennsylvania's Bucks County, the latter residence being shared with painter Joseph Glasco. The success of Goyen's first drama led him to attempt more playwriting: *The Diamond Rattler* had its premiere at the Charles Playhouse in Boston in the spring of 1960. (A television play, *A Possibility of Oil,* had appeared on CBS's "Four Star Theatre" in 1958, with Miss Joan Fontaine in the lead. This play had in it a good deal of material from the story "Rhody's Path," and a better play, *The Diamond Rattler,* grew out of it.)

During this period Goyen also continued to work on the ill-fated novel *Half a Look of Cain,* portions of which he published in *Saturday Evening Post* and in *Southwest Review,* but never as a novel. He did, in another financially bad time, sell the rights for a German translation. But Ernst Robert Curtius died before completing the translation, and the right man to finish it evidently was never found. Those portions of the book which Goyen had published as stories he reprints in his *Collected Stories:* "The Rescue," "The Enchanted Nurse," and "Figure Over the Town." They are among his most fantastical and exciting writings, and lead us to yearn for the whole book. Yet Goyen saw it as his "splendid failure" in a letter addressed to this writer,[30] and as late as 1970 he expressed dissatisfaction with it in a letter to Clyde Grimm: "I am not satisfied with it and my American publisher, Random House, was not, either. I am still struggling with it and cannot yet get it right. Anyway, I'm not anxious to have it published until it's right."[31] Perhaps someday Goyen will complete the book.

One aspect of Goyen's talent which has been uncelebrated is his ability as a song and lyric writer. Among those songs which have been produced is a long ballad called "The Left-handed Boy," which was sung over the film *The Left-Handed Gun,* starring Paul Newman and produced by Warner Brothers. It was Arthur Penn's first film, and as such now enjoys an underground reputation and can be seen on television. Working closely with Penn and the film's producer, Fred Coe, Goyen wrote a ballad which contributed to the success of a film which is now considered by some to be a curious, primitive masterpiece, a forerunner of contemporary films such as *Easy Rider* and *Butch Cassidy and the Sundance Kid*. Goyen's other song-writing projects include the scores for his 1969 production of *The House of Breath* and for the full-scale musical *Aimee!* produced by the Trinity Square Repertory Company in 1974.

In 1962 Goyen was engaged in helping produce the fourth of his plays, *Christy*, at the Actors' Studio. Playing the role of Sue Emma Starnes was the talented actress Doris Roberts—who at this time was greatly admired by other thespians, but had not yet achieved the wide public recognition which was hers a decade later, for her Broadway performances in such plays as *The Secret Affairs of Mildred Wild*, *The Last of the Red-Hot Lovers*, *Cheaters* and *Bad Habits*. Goyen and Miss Roberts were together constantly during the rehearsals and performances of *Christy* (in 1964 they were together, in the American Place Theatre production of that play), and when he once again contracted a bad case of wanderlust, and packed off for Germany, Miss Roberts began to correspond with him.

Her letters were a valued link with reality and the world of New York. Alone in a foreign country, Goyen traveled as a guest of the U.S. State Department for several months, reading in English from his books at universities and at "Amerika Hausen." Young people followed him everywhere, shouting after him *"Dichter! Dichter!"* (Poet! Poet!). Goyen found that both *The House of Breath* and *In a Farther Country* were popular paperbacks in Germany, a fact sadly contrasting with the situation in America, where all his books were out of print. There was, in fact, never an American paperback edition of any one of his books until 1974, twenty-four years after his first book was published.

A highlight of Goyen's trip was to be a reunion with his old translator and champion, Curtius. Goyen wired ahead the date and time of his arrival in the tiny Swiss village where the critic lived. After a long journey, Goyen disembarked from the train to be met by a stranger, come to tell him the old man had suffered a severe stroke. It was one of the shocks of Goyen's adult life: "I had needed so much—desperately—to be with him, to *talk*, to share quandaries and enigmas about literature, the life-of-writing, poetry. When I got to him in a small, dismal Alpine village, I found him speechless—he had suffered the stroke that took his life a few months later. But *I* talked and talked all one day and night, and he nodded, like a mechanical doll."[32] Goyen never knew if the old man understood a word. This situation of the writer endlessly talking to a dumb and possibly deaf Ideal Reader seems all too symbolic for the career of William Goyen and other serious writers.

III   *Middle Years*

Depressed and alone, without the special insights into his own work Curtius had said he had been eager to impart to him, Goyen returned to America. It was 1963, and on November 10 of that year he married Doris Roberts. It is a marriage which has lasted to this day, and of it the author has declared, "My marriage? It's one of my best books!"[33] If the comic plot and characterizations of *The Fair Sister*, his 1963 novel, are any indications of the effect the marriage had upon his spirits at the time, there can be no doubt of his happiness. The former brooding had turned into sheer celebration. During the fall of that year and into the spring of 1964, Goyen worked with the Lincoln Center Repertory Company as the recipient of a Ford Foundation Grant for novelists working in the theater. He and his new wife and stepson, Michael Cannata, moved into a big, rent-controlled apartment on West End Avenue in Manhattan, which his bride furnished beautifully years later with proceeds from her first big Broadway role, in Neil Simon's *The Last of the Red-Hot Lovers*. It was in this apartment Goyen began a series of memoirs, still unpublished, then titled *Six Women*. The six included portraits of Frieda Lawrence, Margo Jones, Mabel Dodge Luhan, Dorothy Brett, Katherine Anne Porter, and an obscure landlady Goyen once knew. In 1975 he was still working on these memoirs, visiting his own papers at the Woodson Research Center of Rice University—the depository for his manuscripts, letters, and photos.

In 1966 Goyen made a decision which was radically to change his life over the next years. He accepted the position of Senior Trade Editor for McGraw-Hill, the large New York book publisher. Goyen had never before been tied to a desk or to business hours. His fictions had been produced on his own schedule, often at the cost of great internal stress. Presumably he felt he could have an editing career and a writing career. (T. S. Eliot was a banker; Wallace Stevens, an insurance executive; William Carlos Williams, a doctor.) But these were the exceptions, not the rule. Not much good came out of Goyen's affiliation with McGraw-Hill. All his life he had been reading manuscripts of others, trying to see the fine ones published. Presumably he enjoyed this role as editor, seeing into print books by such authors as Elizabeth Spencer and Catherine Marshall. He discovered eleven young novelists for the firm, including Michael Rubin and Ann Roiphe. And he was responsible for the firm's keeping in print the books of Henrich Böll, who later was to win the Nobel Prize for Literature.

On the other hand, between 1966 and October 1971, Goyen published *nothing* of his own. On that day, he sent out to all literary agents with whom he had, as editor, been dealing, the following letter: "This is just an official little note advising you that I will no longer be with McGraw-Hill after November first. I am leaving for a time in order to do some of my own work; after that we will see what happens. . . . I will miss our professional relationship as editor and agent, but surely our long-term friendship will continue."[34]

What had happened was simply this: after a long dry spell, Goyen had been absolutely possessed to write his book of Jesus, and the job simply did not allow the hours or the energy. He took the writing of this first nonfiction work every bit as seriously as he did his earlier novels: "I'm quite crazy with so much coming into me—I'm strong, but I've *got* to understand why He did what He did that last week."[35]

A Book of Jesus was completed late in 1971. Originally scheduled for publication at Christmastime of 1972, it finally appeared during Easter Week of 1973. It began what I think of as the second great period in Goyen's productivity. It was followed by the novel *Come, the Restorer;* the *Selected Writings of William Goyen;* and the play *Aimee!*—all in 1974. In 1975 the twenty-fifth-anniversary-edition of *The House of Breath*, with a new preface, appeared, as well as the impressive volume *Collected Stories of William Goyen*, a book containing twenty-five stories, a novella, and an author's preface. It is a book which will be read for decades to come. In 1976 his early poems were reprinted as *Nine Poems*.

Today William Goyen divides his time between Manhattan—in that West End Avenue apartment which he and his wife have filled with books and green plants and theater memorabilia—and Los Angeles—where they live in a large, Spanish-looking home in the Hollywood Hills. It was his wife's work in films and television which first took them to the Coast, but he has adjusted to the change. Whether in Los Angeles or New York, Goyen rises early, early as a rooster, and retires to his den to write every morning. He needs and demands absolute silence. As always, he avoids the literary Establishment. For Goyen is not in love with the business of being a writer; he is in love with the act of writing. Too many confuse the two. He admits to disappointment over his lack of recognition, and calls his sixtieth year, the year of publication of his *Collected Stories,* "a just-about totally negative year."[36] Despite excellent reviews— the book was highly praised, for example, by Joyce Carol Oates in the *New York Times Book Review*—his *Collected Stories* received no awards. It was not, in fact, even among the nominees for the National Book Award or the National Book Critics Circle Award. Goyen has yet to be asked to join the National Institute of Arts and Letters.

Nevertheless, his work prevails. "What I wanted was to make splendor," he wrote in retrospect of his life. And every day, he does. "I can't imagine *not* writing," he has said. "Writing simply is a way of life for me. The older I get, the more of a way of life it is. At the beginning, it was totally a way of life excluding everything else. Now it's gathered to it marriage and children and other responsibilities. But still, it is simply a way of life before all other ways, a way to observe the world and to move through life, among human beings, and to record it all above all and to shape it, to give it sense, and to express something of myself in it. Writing is something I cannot imagine living without, nor scarcely would want to. Not to live daily as a writing person is inconceivable to me."[37]

CHAPTER 2

The House of Breath

I *The World of Goyen's Imagination*

SOME writers achieve their mature "style" (which is often more a matter of content than of imagery or sentence structure) through a long evolution. An extreme example is James Joyce, who began with the naturalism of *Dubliners*, proceeded to write the poetic *Portrait of the Artist as a Young Man*, then the mythic and wildly funny *Ulysses*, and finally arrived at *Finnegans Wake*, in which he attempted to create a vision and language all his own. Not so with William Goyen. Goyen's manner and content were fully developed from the first page of his first book onward. He published, in fact, surprisingly little before that first book, *The House of Breath* (1950). But once having found his subject and style, the book seems to have sprung full panoplied from his psyche, like Minerva from the head of Zeus.

And what an original book it is! *The House of Breath* is unique in our literature, owing no debts to any literary antecedents. One reason for such uniqueness is that Goyen almost always writes in the first-person singular, and the voice is unquestionably his own— Southwestern, sensitive, searching, deeply rooted in Old Testament locutions. Goyen, exiled in body from the Southwest, can never absent himself from that locale. He has the almost morbid sensibility that comes from the feelings of exile and suppression. Of his work, we can say when we read him, "Nobody could have written this except Goyen." His southernness, his religion, his sense of relationship, the impressions of his childhood, pervade everything he writes. In his books the man who speaks is not a prophet, clothed with thunder, but a seer who tries to understand. He has chosen to write with the most fundamental part of his being as a writer; and for all his irony and humor (very little of the latter is found in *The House of Breath*, however), we never doubt of the depth of his feelings. Indeed, the depth of his feelings is the one thing above all else one remembers about his books.

A second reason his work is unique is that his books seem composed through a sort of double process—that of the photograph and that of the poem of the fact and the vision. Like Turgenev, Goyen does not seem to see his books as a succession of *events*. Rather, they are perceived as a succession of *emotions* radiating from some central figure. Each individual section of his novel concerns a different character, each of whom acts as a magnet which has the power to draw disparate things, apparently incongruous, together. The connection, as Virginia Woolf said of Turgenev's novels, is

not of events but of emotions, and if at the end of the book we feel a sense of completeness, it must be that in spite of his defects as a storyteller Turgenev's ear for emotion was so fine that even if he uses an abrupt contrast, or passes away from his people to a description of the sky or of the forest, all is held together by the truth of his insight. . . . It is for this reason that his novels are not merely symmetrical but make us feel so intensely."[1]

These words are totally appropriate for Goyen, who is such an insightful writer that he manages to make a major character of the river in this first novel, of a fowl in his story *The White Rooster*, of a snake in *Come, the Restorer*. Whether sister or snake, we care for Goyen's characters because they are not represented as the *whole* of life, but merely as *part* of the whole. His people seem profoundly conscious of their relation to all things outside themselves. As Turgenev's Elena asks in her diary, "What is my youth for, what am I living for, why have I a soul, what is it all for?" so too Goyen's Aunt Malley Ganchion keeps asking, "What kin are we all to each other, anyway?"

Thirdly, Goyen's imagery is often dreamlike, unreal to the point of surrealism, and always intensely personal. He draws upon a personal mythology of rattlesnakes and oil wells, tightrope walkers and flagpole sitters, which is distinctly his own. Goyen is in point a fabulist, making his own myths and creating characters much larger than life. His dreamlike imagery and mythic characters are but two facets of his distinctive style. His stories and novels are all written in prose, but in prose which has many of the characteristics of poetry. It is a style which yokes the exaltations of poetry with the ordinariness of spoken prose. His books are dramatic, but they are not plays.

Like poetry, they give the outlines of life rather than the whole of it (as in many novels). In this respect, Goyen's fiction bears little relationship to the sociological novel, or the novel of environment. It is precisely for this reason he cannot be labeled a "regional writer," despite the fact that the action of most of the books occurs in Southwest Texas. As quoted earlier, the author addressed himself to just that accusation in a note in 1955, in which he concluded, "The themes of my work have no affinity with the eccentricites of Southern personality or Gothic bizarreries, though my work has been attracted into that category through spurious association."[2] Indeed, Goyen is neither regional nor naturalistic because he is so interested in giving not only the relationship of people to the land, or to one another, but also the relationship of their minds to one another as well as to large general ideas and past traditions and influences. As Virginia Woolf said in another essay,

We have come to forget that a large and important part of life consists in our emotions toward such things as roses and nightingales, the dawn, the sunset, life, death, and fate; we forget that we spend much time sleeping, dreaming, thinking, reading, alone; we are not entirely occupied in personal relations; all our energies are not absorbed in making our livings . . . we long for some more impersonal relationship. We long for ideas, for dreams, for imaginations, for poetry.[3]

That was Virginia Woolf writing in 1927. In 1950 Goyen's first novel revealed a sensibility and a method sympathetic with those longings. Goyen's was an early example of the "poetic novel"—that is, a novel which approaches the search for reality by discarding realism. The genre also has been called, by Anaïs Nin, "the Novel of the Future," a term applied to those novels, like Goyen's, which strive to unite and synthesize various forms of reality (drama and action, past and present, personal and collective), eschewing the literalness of prose for the dimensionalization of poetry. Accordingly, Goyen's novels break with the things which *are* in order to merge with those things which *may be*, including even spirits, which figure prominently in his second book, *Ghost and Flesh*. Goyen's aim is not to state a concrete truth, but to express a poetic truth. And, as Elizabeth Bowen posits in her "Notes on Writing a Novel," "The essence of a poetic truth is that no statement of it can be final."[4]

That is precisely why Goyen's novels are so rewarding, why his admirers reread them year after year: because there is no final "meaning" to be found in them. His stories and "novels" (which he once, quite accurately, called "Romances", in the Hawthornian sense) move forward by a chronology of emotions, not of dates. Like Virginia Woolf in her own novels, Goyen consciously or unconsciously sought to bring to the novel not the familiar character structure, but the visionary insights of a poet. Chances are, it was an unintentional choice: Does one ever deliberately set out to be a poet? Yet a few of our novelists are just that. Goyen, and Woolf and Miss Nin take it upon themselves to express what we ourselves cannot express. They attempt to show us that our lives do not occur on only the linear level, but simultaneously on several. As Miss Nin has written, "What we are accustomed to accepting as familiar is the external appearance of reality. *The external story is what I consider unreal.*"[5]

America, of course, has long shunned her poets, and held as suspect anyone with a lyrical bent, considering them unstable rather than imaginative. Even sophisticated book reviewers have not quite known what to make of Goyen's fiction. In the pages of the *New York Times Book Review* the southern novelist Shirley Ann Grau pronounced Goyen's ecological masterpiece, *Come, the Restorer*, "foolish." A weekly news magazine said of his *In a Farther Country*, "God knows Mr. Goyen must think this is art, because he surely didn't write it to make money."

Yet from the first Goyen chose to abandon the conventional, and surely the commercial, novel, in favor of embracing instead the private world of fantasy and imagination, those essential but neglected parts of our own reality. If Goyen's work goes against the American grain, it is because, as Miss Nin says, "Our American culture decided at one point to trust the 'objective' vision of the many against the one, the 'subjective.'" It is precisely for that reason Miss Nin feels Goyen's work is essential to our time: "I would suggest to young writers the study of all of William Goyen's books, for a poetry born of the earth and which welds the physical world to the emotional world. In his writing the two are perfectly synchronized, flesh and emotion, dream and human experience."[6]

Goyen, then, is an American poet of atmosphere, climate, mood, and subtle exchanges. He charts our inner as well as our outer weather, in books which fuse reality, illusion, and dream. Among the most significant of these is his first, *The House of Breath*, a book which has proven to be a modern classic because it enriches the human mind, actually adding to its treasures. One discovers in it unmistakable moral truths and recaptures eternal passions of the human heart. And Goyen expresses his discoveries in a form at once great and sweeping, subtle and yet sensible, poetic and beautiful in itself. The novel speaks to all who come to it in a style of Goyen's own, which happens also to be that of common speech, a style new but without neologisms, new and old at the same time, timeless as the Old Testament stories, easily acceptable to any age.

II *Entrances to* The House of Breath

The House of Breath is a book so rich, so original, that even a quarter of a century after publication there is little agreement on its "meaning" and implications. For instance, Daniel Stern has seen it as being in the tradition of the Southern Gothic, a novel dealing with madness, disintegration of a great family, and the grotesque.[7] Gerald Ashford, on the other hand, reads it as no novel at all, but a long poem.[8] Louise Y. Gossett cites it as a novel on the breaking apart of the modern world.[9] But Anais Nin, predictably, terms it a synchronization of dream and human experience,[10] an opinion shared by Gaston Bachelard, who thought it a novel on the unreality of reality.[11] The German critic Ernst R. Curtius believed it to be an epic on alienation,[12] while Frenchman Michel Lucazeau thinks it an example of "the first grade of Surrealism."[13]

Surely Goyen's 181-page book cannot be all these things . . . or can it? Certain critics have found its ultimate meaning totally elusive. Charles White, for instance, declared in exasperation, "Mr. Goyen, in some of his more ecstatic moments, soars beyond the reaches of ordinary mortals."[14] Nonsense. Rather than being incomprehensible, *The House of Breath* is a novel shimmering with so many implications and resonances that it requires many readings before comprehension. Even then, there can be no one "meaning" or interpretation.

One feature of the books in this series for which I write has been to offer a plot summary of each of the author's major books, a recording of the book's action. With *The House of Breath* this is exceedingly difficult to do. It is somewhat like attempting a plot summary of *The Sound and the Fury*, or *Ulysses*, or *Finnegans Wake*. Goyen's novel is subjective to the point of being plotless.

The "action" of *The House of Breath* takes place in a moment within a person's head. In this moment the life of the person (the narrator) flows into and out of a stream of persons, places, things, creatures, rivers—all nature, finally. A whole history momentarily bursts alive, illuminated. It is the very breath of the narrator that recreates, in its calling out in this moment of despair, an entire lost world. It is in this apocalyptic moment that "everything flows into everything" (to quote from the novel). A town and a family are momentarily restored.

The work is visionary, yet constructed with common speech, the folk speech (superstition, image, song, game) of people of rural East Texas. An elegance and grace of language results which is closer to that of Proust, T. S. Eliot, and Lawrence, than to regional literature.

The House of Breath is cast in the form of an autobiography in which, nevertheless, the narrator himself plays a role not much more substantial than that of his many other characters. Indeed, as Patrice Repusseau maintains in his unpublished thesis, *An Approach to The House of Breath*, there are times when one is uncertain, can never be certain, just who the "narrator" is. At times we are given a sensibility, and a sensibility only, talking. A novel about the quest for identity, *The House of Breath* examines the lives of those who touched the narrator most deeply; in realizing their lives, he feels he will realize himself.

Externally the novel's method is one in which the normal chronological narrative order is often subordinated to a quasi-musical arrangement of material by means of which similar or antithetical persons, situations, and moods are rhythmically balanced against one another to create a pattern which does not depend upon the order of time, but rather upon the sense of likeness (kinship), of synchronicity (to use Jung's term). At the same time, every scene or character presented is dominated by Goyen's obsession with the need to recapture past time and past emotion. The narrator's identity can reveal itself to himself only when he understands how he relates (in both senses of that word) to those who were around him in his formative years.

It should be apparent from the above that *The House of Breath* resembles, in some conceptual and technical ways, that other great novel of nostalgia and sensations, Proust's *Remembrance of Things Past*. Goyen's novel is, of course, more modest than that massive, seven-volume "apologia pro vita sua" of Proust's. The latter author attempts to recall and examine an entire society; Goyen largely is concerned with recapturing the past of one family in one town.

But there are resemblances. Both artists were obsessed with rescuing something from the flux, of establishing in the eternity of art those ephemeral experiences which each had undergone or observed and which, often in the most subtle ways, had changed his life. In both cases memory serves as the bridge between the past as lived and the art as recreation, between the past self and the present self. (Goyen literally uses a bridge as symbol in this sense in his later story "Bridge of Music, River of Sand.").

Another comparison comes to mind: *The House of Breath* is a memory-novel in the way Tennessee Williams's *The Glass Menagerie* is a memory-play. Goyen attempts to recapture the essence of the lives of the many family members who occupied the house of boyhood. Three family surnames are especially prominent: the Ganchion and Starnes families, and the Clegg family. All the members of one family are related to the others, though the familial links are not readily apparent at times, and it is up to the reader to trace them. (Some future edition or reprinting of the novel might be well served by appending a genealogy, as Malcolm Cowley convinced Faulkner to append to the *Portable* edition of his own works. Such a genealogy for *The House of Breath* has been worked out by the French critic Patrice Repusseau in his admirable thesis.)

The structure of this memory-novel is a simple one: the narrator, in a moment of despair, mentally returns to the world of his childhood. He invokes all his relations and companions and even familiar elements of the natural world. Chapter One introduces the sensibility of the narrator and establishes his despair. The voice of the narrator then opens each subsequent chapter by introducing a new character or a new memory. The breath of the narrator is the medium for building the entire world, as Repusseau has shown. In retelling the old stories of his childhood, William Goyen is searching out his roots in the white world as did Alex Haley for his black ones in his book *Roots*.

Goyen's second chapter introduces, poetically, the house that held all these people and memories together. Chapter Two is more objective in its descriptions, and introduces more characters: Aunty, Uncle Jimbob, Aunt Malley, Uncle Walter Warren, Christy (a young man who is a central character in the novel), Granny Ganchion, and all the cousins: Sue Emma (called Swimma), Follie (an alter-ego for the narrator), Berryben, Jessy, Maidie, and Miss Hattie Clegg.

After these chapters, individual voices of the various relatives take over succeeding chapters, telling their individual (and often complicated) stories in Chapters Four through Eleven. Christy speaks to us in Chapters Five and Twelve; Aunty in Chapter Six; Hattie Clegg in Eight; Malley, Jessy, and Berryben in Nine; Folner in Ten (in one of the book's most gorgeous and heartbreaking sequences); Old Fuzz and Granny in Eleven. The storytelling is not limited to humans. In Chapter Four the river has a story to tell. In Chapter Seven we hear the voice of the well. Then in Chapter Eleven the narrator's voice predominates once again, in the longest chapter in the novel. Chapter Thirteen shifts focus to the reality of Chapter One, bringing the book, and memory, around full circle.

As with the next novel Goyen was to write, *In a Farther Country*, the chapters of this first novel are so many beads on a chain, a clasped chain forming a circle. Goyen himself was aware of this structure. It is a part of his very world-view: "Something in the world links faces and leaves and rivers and woods and wind together and makes of them a string of medallions with all our faces on them, worn forever round our necks, kin."[15]

Repusseau has commented also on the novel's structure in this way: "The form which perfectly fits the general structure of the book is the form of a rosary. We can say that that structure of *The House of Breath* is a 'rosary structure.' This is suggested to us by the text itself and at the very beginning of the book." M. Repusseau then quotes from Goyen's text:

I began to name over and over in my memory every beautiful and loved image I ever had, to name and praise them over and over like a rosary, bead by bead, saying, Granny Ganchion, I touch you and name you; Folner, I touch you and name you, Aunty, Malley, Swimma, Boy, I touch you and name you and claim you all.[16]

To help the reader of this complicated work, I suggest two entrances to Goyen's house of breath, two ways of seeing the materials the author has ordered, ways of sharing his intentions and vision. The first is a matter of secrets kept by each main character. In a somewhat plotless novel, one in which chapters are mere refractions of the teller's memory, the revelation of a secret (or secrets) by each protagonist is an important dramatic element uniting the book, and one which no critic has before touched upon. Indeed, "everything in this world is not black and white," as Goyen instructs us at one point. And it is the gray areas—the unclear, the undifferentiated, the secret—which he explores most extensively.

There is, to begin with, the secret of the narrator-as-a-young-boy, a character simply called Boy. His secret is that, at least physically, he is losing his boyhood; unperceived, he is growing a bush of pubic hair, which Christy threatens to, but does not, expose. In the course of human events, this is a seemingly minor secret, and a common one. Except that the entire novel throbs with pubescent lust, and Boy's adjustment to, and later denial of, Christy is the core of the novel. It is Christy's ambiguous sexual intentions toward Boy which prompts him to take stock of his own situation, and to leave the house, to declare: "I will get up now and go now, where I belong, and be what I must be"—a declaration as central to the book's meaning as Stephen Dedalus's is to Joyce's *Portrait*: "Welcome, O Life! I go to encounter for the millionth time the reality of experience and to forge in the smithy of my soul the uncreated conscience of my race."

The next two secrets involve ill health. Walter Warren Starnes (who also kept his membership in the Ku Klux Klan secret from all but fellow members, till his limping form beneath the sheet identified him for the narrator) died of a cancer and kept its presence unknown until the autopsy. And Jessy Ganchion died from a liver disease, the pains of which she also kept private. She would not dis-ease the world with her disease. These fatal maladies, plus the various cysts, fistules, goiters, and congenital malformities catalogued in the novel (including two hydrocephalic babies and one "frog boy") can be seen as manifestations of moral as well as physical decay in a world gone wrong once avarice dominates over *agape*.

The fourth secret is more spectacular—the revelation, once Christy's brother Folner dies and his trunks are unpacked and boa feathers and sequins are revealed—that "Follie" was a female-impersonator, a transvestite. His suicide underscores a point already made by the decline of Sue Emma Starnes: that those who run away from the house, away from the town of Charity, fail to find happiness just as miserably as do those who remain behind. The brothers Folner and Christy are male counterparts of Arnold Bennett's Sophia and Constance, in *The Old Wives' Tale*—one sophisticated and city-bound, one constant and home-tied, both incomplete in the end.

Perhaps even more shocking is the revelation that Granny Gan-

chion conceived Christy by a circus gypsy, and that her husband was
not Christy's father at all. (Somewhat ambiguous in the novel,
Granny's secret was given greater emphasis in the 1969 Trinity
Square Playhouse production of Goyen's play version of the book,
completely rewritten by Goyen for the stage.) Christy's conception
through an unseen father heightens the Christly comparisons already apparent in his name, his exile, and his long suffering. It also
helps answer the novel's refrain, "What kin are we all to each other,
anyway?" We are at once related and distant. For Granny, the
moment of Christy's conception was the only real experience of her
life, and one she will choose to relive in memory time and again.
(Goyen's preoccupation with the Christ figure resulted, over twenty
years later, in his writing a nonfictional study, *A Book of Jesus*.)

Then there is the scene which is, for most readers, the high point
of the novel, Christy's confession to Boy of the secret absence of sex
from his marriage to Otey, and their subsequent strange but beautiful consummation under water when he dived to save her from
drowning. In the act of losing Otey he was saved. In the act of
drowning, she was rescued. In Christy's one act of having to lower
himself to find a meaning, he perceived a truth to last a lifetime.

So many secrets hidden from one another beneath the roof of one
house! Even the river, a true presence in the novel, has a story it
keeps all to itself, refusing to give up the body of Selmers Chubb, or
even to tell what happened to it. All these secrets, these hidden
aspirations, are clues to motivation and therefore to the book's final
meaning.

While the secrets are clandestine, certain symbols and symbolic
acts within the novel are very open. They need only be pondered to
be understood, and, once understood, to contribute to understanding. For the most part, Goyen's symbols are highly elemental—invoking air, earth, and water for association. (In *Come, the Restorer*
he adds the fourth element, fire, while maintaining the other three.)

Since water imagery and symbolism predominate in *The House of
Breath*, they will be considered first, beginning with Boy's descent
into the well in order to clean it. In Freudian terms, the well shaft
could be a Yoni symbol, signifying that, in his search for self, Boy
has entered the region of the feminine. But more likely a Christian
interpretation is implied, with his act of cleansing the well an attempt to keep his own purity, since the well of refreshing water is
always associated with salvation in Christian symbolism.

Certainly Christy's descent into the river to save Otey is a redemptive act. When Christy surfaces to the light of this world, he is enlightened to the world as well. Christy-Christ has found a peace which passes understanding. As Curtius wrote, "The harmony with the elemental power of earth operates in this book as a stream that washes away all stains, that purifies and heals."[17]

If the well and the river are positive water symbols, the iced-over ditch in which Roma, the cow, is sacrificed is a negative one. Since water itself signifies the life force and all potentialities, it follows that ice is the very stultification of life. And since the cow in nearly all world cultures represents the primal principle of abundance—from her function of nourishing the world with her milk—the cow in the ditch becomes a symbol of the female principle (such as the Mother of Waters). Moreover, Goyen's is almost a sacred cow, named for Rome, mother-seat of the church and world-navel of Christianity.

Thus, when Christy shoots Roma, he first enacts a blood ritual, a rite of initiation for Boy. But he also symbolically destroys the female principle. All that would seem to remain is the world of manly camaraderie—with perhaps homosexual overtones. In such a world Boy may not become a true man. This is seen when the destruction of the cow (passive/female) is followed by the destruction of the snake (active/male): "a purple snake glided over my image and Christy shot it, tearing my image into pieces" (p. 172). On one level, the snake is the personification of evil, as in the Garden of Eden myth. When Boy's reflection is crossed by it, we are shown him torn by depravity. But here a Freudian rather than a Christian reading seems more appropriate, with the snake as phallic symbol, Boy's manliness dismembered. Being purple, it is doubly phallic, with that color (the hue of the imperial Roman paludament, as well as the Cardinal's) representing power.

So with Christy's shooting of the snake, Boy's self-image literally is destroyed. His state of fallen grace is reinforced by the symbol of the fallen dove in the wood—embodiment of Boy's fall from innocence or grace. The fallen dove, in turn, is related to the wreath of bloody birds which is an emblem of initiation but also of Christy's message of carnality to Boy. Inhabitants of the loftier element, air, and thereby symbolic of the higher aspirations, the dead birds whose swinging beaks peck the boy's flesh are a hair shirt, reminders of his own spiritual debasement. Boy is left now with two

choices: to remain a boy forever, and stick by Christy—who by his
own admission served as a mother rather than brother to the
homosexual Folner, saying, "Makes me part woman and I know it
and I'll never get over it" (p. 149); or, to leave Charity. When Boy
chooses the latter course, rejection becomes a new beginning toward selfhood. As Curtius observes, "The law of separation and
reunion also prevails throughout Goyen's book."[18]

While Boy and Christy both seek self-knowledge in water,
Granny Ganchion's quest is conducted below ground, in the basement where she sits amongst all her canned fruit (preserves) and
attempts to preserve her past as well by fondling a string of cheap
red beads given her by the gypsy lover. The basement into which
she descends is expressive of the psychological unconscious which
she plumbs and which she conceals from the legions of Ganchions
and Starnses overhead. Like the medieval cave of Jungian psychology, it also symbolizes security and the impregnability of the unconscious.

The color of the beads and the contents of the jars might also be
signifiers. Red intuitively is the color of pulsing blood and of fire, of
surging and tearing emotions, the very emotions Granny wishes to
invoke. Fruit, further, traditionally is a symbol of earthly desire and
of origins, being seeded at the center (as Granny herself was seeded
at the center by the Gypsy). So this silent old creature, sitting alone,
says her beads in a near-religious rite, surrounded by symbols of her
one earthly act of defiance and lust.

The House of Breath purports to be a lyric epic of the town of
Charity and the region of East Texas. Yet three additional symbols
alone indicate wider implications. The first is the cistern wheel,
which seems the world axis around which the family members re-
volve, coming and going, ever drawn toward the center. Another is
the world map in the kitchen, its countries resembling so many
dissected chicken parts. The map belongs to Christy and seems an
image for the discontinuity of his world, his psyche fragmented
rather than whole. And yet it is a picture of the world. In the small
town of Charity, Boy has had an intuitive apprehension of the wide
world and known himself to be a part of it. Finally there is the
picture in the hall of the blinded girl sitting on a blue world, playing
a lyre. She functions clearly as the house Muse, one of the daughters
of Memory. Yet it is appropriate that the Muse is blind—unwhole,

nonvisionary. Ambition and lust have torn the house of breath—which is at once the human form as well as the abode—asunder, and it remains a splendid but surely a fallen house.

CHAPTER 3

Ghost and Flesh

I *Individuation*

IF *The House of Breath* presents, among other themes, the necessity for a young man to break with the past, Goyen's second book, *Ghost and Flesh,* is an eight-part work depicting the ceaseless conflict between past and present, invisible and visible. A group of eight extraordinary stories, obviously written as a book with a common theme and unique symbols, rather than having merely been "collected," *Ghost and Flesh* deals with simple, compassionate people, men and women, each driven by a need to reach beyond and outside themselves to find in life some sort of absolute truth. As the critic William Peden states, the characters

are dominated or victimized by what the author seems to consider the tyrannies of the past, of tradition, of sex, and of an all-encompassing, nameless fear. They search for a means of effecting some kind of satisfactory compromise between past and present; they struggle to believe that life and death, the visible and the invisible, are factors in a continuous chain of being which is existence.[1]

Another major theme of the book is the failure to communicate. (In one story a message at the end of a kite breaks loose and flies away to wherever it is words are unseen!) In story after story, one sign of man's isolation from himself and from others is the ghost. Goyen's use of the ghost often corresponds with the idea of the ghost or revenant—some shade of a lost culture or a guilt appearing out of the past—as often found in Irish literature. Ghosts also serve as symbols for all we have lost, which demand recognition still. Story after story records a great struggle for wholeness, what Jung would call individuation. Goyen's characters' waking and dream lives create a meandering pattern in which individual strands become

46

visible, then vanish, then return again. A meandering design of dust and water, ghost and flesh, dismemberment and wholeness, mechanical and human, lost and found, ultimately reveals in the characters a process of psychic growth—the process of individuation.

As related as their themes and symbols may be, the stories reveal widely varying styles, from the very straightforward narrative of "The White Rooster" to the shifting focuses in "Pore Perrie." The latter is an example of Goyen's point of view which might be called multiple refraction,[2] a technique which further serves to reveal the isolation of the individual.

II   *"The White Rooster"*

The first story in this first book of Goyen's stories is still one of his most famous. "The White Rooster" is frequently anthologized and was even made into an experimental film. The late Frederick J. Hoffman, in *The Art of Southern Fiction*, cited it for its "fineness of comic perception and a precision that place it very high on an already distinguished list of short fiction in Southern literature."[3]

Numerous other critics have discussed the story as well, but all seem to miss the point. Peden, for instance, has called it "essentially realistic,"[4] and Louise Y. Gossett interprets "The White Rooster" as a dramatization of "the conflict of generations." She sees Grandpa Samuels's orgy of violence at the conclusion as "a startling comment on the fury of age. It is as if the past, feeling itself threatened, turned in an insane rage to demolish the present."[5]

But "The White Rooster" is not a realistic story, but rather a Western tall tale on one level and an allegory on another. Mrs. Gossett's interpretation of the allegory as the battle of the generations is incorrect. It is, rather, the battle of the sexes that Goyen dramatizes. Mrs. Marcy Samuels is the author's prototype of the emasculating female. Described from essentially a misogynist's point of view, she is "a terrible sight to any barnyard creature, her hair like a big bush and her terrible bosom heaving and falling, her hands thrashing the air." Later she is described with "her full-blown buttocks protruding like a monstrous flower in bud." Marcy already has rendered her husband, Watson, ineffectual and cowardly, and at the time of the story he is reduced to a "slow, patient little man."

Having conquered Watson, Marcy turns her ambitions toward Grandpa Samuels and, by extension, to the white rooster: in her obsession the two figures have become one. The rooster, of course, is a traditional male symbol. Now, with tired body and torn feathers, it is a figure of the pursued male. When the rooster violates Marcy's pansy patch, it is the violation of her feminine psyche by the male. And when Grandpa Samuels defends the rooster, he is defending the honor and the supremacy of his sex: "Don't you know there's something in a rooster that won't be downed? Don't you know there's some creatures won't be dead easily?" But Marcy, determined, replies: "All you have to do is wring their necks."

Goyen, then, has staged his battle of the sexes on the symbolic level, in the conflict between the rooster and Marcy, as well as on the literal level, between Grandpa Samuels and Marcy. To reinforce his theme, moreover, he has borrowed heavily, I suggest, from the biblical legend of Samson and Delilah as a controlling framework for his story. (Goyen appropriates archetypal figures from world literature to underscore the point of certain others of his stories as well: Son Wanger in "Poor Perrie," whose dark complexion, rumored Semitic blood, and unfulfilled quest, recall the figure of the Wandering Jew; and George Kurunus, the freak in the midst of beauty who crowns himself King of the May in "The Grasshopper's Burden," recalls the Hunchback of Notre Dame, both in his symbolic deformity and in his symbolic act.)

Grandpa Samuels, of course, is the Samson figure, his last name one clue to his legendary role. He is the figure of the incapacitated male at the mercy of a female in league with the Philistines. Like the biblical Samson, Grandpa Samuels has been a wanderer and is at times capable of great displays of physical stamina, but intellectually and morally he is weak. Like Samson when he entered Delilah's life, Grandpa Samuels was in good health when he came to live with Marcy, and "would probably live long." Yet before the second year is over, he "fell thin." Goyen does not give us a cause for Grandpa Samuels's fast failing; yet within the context of the story, we can assume it is due to the corrupting influence of Marcy herself.

When Marcy lies in wait to torment Granda Samuels and to strangle the white rooster, she is like the Gazites lying in wait for Samson. Grandpa Samuels's repeated recoveries are Samson's repeated victories over the enemy. When Marcy sets a trap for the rooster, she is Delilah setting a trap for Samson by secretly shearing his hair in the night, an act of symbolic emasculation. When Grandpa Samuels is finally subdued, he becomes the figure of Samson eyeless in Gaza—physically as well as symbolically violated—grinding in the prison house. He restlessly wheels his chair from room to room in Marcy's home, and his confinement to a wheelchair is a symbolic statement of his impotence. The Philistines have captured him at last.

Grandpa Samuels is to have his Samsonian revenge, however. Just as Samson brought down the temple on all his enemies in revenge for his blindness, so too Grandpa Samuels destroys Marcy and her home. Goyen even describes the day of the act in the language of a legend: "All through the home, in every room, there was darkness and doom, the air of horror, slaughter, and utter finish." When Grandpa Samuels destroys the house, he relives the Samson legend and simultaneously exorcises his fear of the tyranny of the female:

And then he wheeled wildly away through the rooms of Marcy Samuels' house, feeling a madness all within him, being liberated, running free. He howled with laughter and rumbled like a runaway carriage through room and room, sometimes coughing in paroxysms. He rolled here and there in every room, destroying everything he could reach, he threw up pots and pans in the kitchen, was in the flour and sugar like a whirlwind, overturned chairs and ripped the upholstery in the living room until the stuffing flew in the air; and covered with straw and flour, white like a demented ghost, he flaying the bedroom wallpaper into hanging shreds; coughing and howling, he lashed and wrecked and razed until he thought he was bringing the very house down upon himself.

The phrase "bringing the very house down upon himself" affirms the probability that Goyen consciously or subconsciously evoked the figure of doomed Samson when he created Samuels.

The Samson legend is fulfilled when Grandpa Samuels himself dies in the destruction of the house. Death through the compulsive act is preferable to living incapacitated and tormented by the female Philistine. The story concludes with the ineffectual Watson standing dumbfounded in the ruins, incapable of the revolt that was the salvation of Samuels's soul, helpless even to understand it, much less to tell others its meaning. Watson is the ultimate victim of Goyen's battle royal of the sexes.

III   *"The Letter in the Cedarchest"*

"The Letter in the Cedarchest" concerns Lucille—one of the

many orphans in the book, and a lady whose husband has left her—
and Little Pigeon, a crazy woman whose sister has left *her*. The two
are opposites: Lucille has nothing, and lives in an unfurnished
house. Little Pigeon, while having no mind, has a house full of
material things. The two of them come together to create a world
of their own in Little Pigeon's house: "The room was so full of
decorations and stuff that there wasn't enough space left in it to cuss
a cat in. There were hanging paper lanterns, paper streamers
streaming from the ceiling, paper balls and paper stars. They had
made a fairyland playhouse out of Little Pigeon's spotless living
room."

There is a parallel here with the "Spain" which Marietta
McGee-Chavez creates in her apartment on West 23rd Street in
New York City, in Goyen's second novel, *In a Farther Country*.
There is in much of his work a design on the part of characters to
reshape their environments into their own images, or into the images of their origins. As the third character in "The Letter in the
Cedarchest," Sammye, says: "All we want, I guess, is a household
that will let us be the way we are." That desire forms the basis of
some of Goyen's best stories. Certainly it is also the theme of "The
Tenant in the Garden," a tale in which a gentle man desires to live
in a tiny playhouse, but will not be left alone to do it by meddlers.
The theme also predominates in "Figure Over the Town," in which
a flagpole sitter figures as a symbol of the artist and the nonconformist.

In "Letter in the Cedarchest" Sammye functions as the protesting
majority. To Little Pigeon, she is nothing more real than a ghost
come to vex her once in a while. But to Sammye, Little Pigeon is a
total preoccupation. Sammye is the outsider who cannot tolerate
such individuality. The life of the imagination is not to be endured.

IV "Pore Perrie"

"Pore Perrie" is a simple tale, but one containing the seeds of a
large theme which was to concern Goyen for decades: the multiple
problems of being another man's son, not one's supposed father's,
when the search for identity, the knowledge of one's true roots, and
the acceptance of responsibilities become preoccupations. (As late
as 1974 Goyen was immersed in these same themes; indeed, the
working title of his novel, *Come, the Restorer*, originally was
Another Man's Son, and the phrase motivates his *Book of Jesus*.)

In "Pore Perrie" we are given Son, an adopted foundling, at the time he learns he is an adopted bastard. Upon receiving this knowledge, he sexually mutilates himself (as does Boney Benson, later in the volume, in the story "A Shape of Light"). It is the ultimate act of rejection of the flesh. Son becomes the eternally homeless, the disinherited, the unsatisfied spiritual seeker. He is not unlike Old Somebody, in the later story "Children of Old Somebody," who also roams the earth searching peace; or even the aforementioned Boney Benson, forever chasing after his chimera; and both can be related to the ghost of Raymond Emmons, in the story "Ghost and Flesh, Water and Dirt," forever revisiting his wife in search of a separate peace. In all these stories Goyen is continually attempting to explore variations on a theme, the impossible quest for unity of the spirit with the flesh.

V   "Ghost and Flesh, Water and Dirt"

"Ghost and Flesh, Water and Dirt," is a soliloquy, in colloquialisms, of Margy Emmons, who at seventeen married a thirty-year-old railroad man who later committed suicide just after their only child, a daughter, died of a riding accident. The principal theme of the story is that one never knows what one possesses until after one has lost it. All of life, Goyen explicitly says here, is a sharing of flesh and ghosts, of present and past, and each of us is composed of as much of the past as we are of the present, and that part which lasts the longest is the past. Moreover, Goyen here insists that there is a world of the spirit as well as of the flesh and tells us we must accept the spirit (ghosts) as easily as we do the flesh. One supplements the other make a full life, and it is the full life which is the life worth living, let alone contemplating.

"Ghost and Flesh, Water and Dirt" is written in language which deliberately attempts to approximate the word as spoken in the Southwest. As Goyen wrote of it in the "Author's Preface" to his *Collected Stories:*

. . . Since the people of the region where most of my stories emanate—or hover over—(they do, I believe, move in and through the great world) are natural talkers and use their speech with gusto and almost operatic delivery; and since the language of their place is rich with phrases and expressions out of the Bible, the Negro imagination, the Mexican fantasy, Deep South Evangelism, the jargon of cottonfield and cotton gin, of oil field, railroad and sawmill, I, coming up among them, had at my ears a glorious sound, and in my hands a marvelous instrument of language, given to me. I worked at this instrument as though it were a fiddle or a cello, to get the music out of it; and I was finally able to hear it almost as a foreign language; and in several of my stories (most notably GHOST AND FLESH, WATER AND DIRT), I have wanted to record as closely as possible the speech as *heard*—as though I were notating music.

VI   "The Grasshopper's Burden"

A "skulled building of stone," in reality a schoolhouse, is a central symbol in "The Grasshopper's Burden," the stone building seeming to the writer not only a microcosm for the world, but a symbol of the skull beneath the flesh. It is a tale of Beauty (the girl Quella) and the Beast (the deformed George Kurunus). Quella represents the egocentric, nonthinking norm. George, with a face "like a grasshopper's face," is all the others are not. A sensitive human, he is seen by the others as no better than an insect: "If the schoolhouse burned it would burn him like a cricket in it." Yet George is symbol of the artist.

Given such prejudice, it is only by disrupting the given order of things (during a fire drill) that the nonconformist can prevail. With all the others out of the schoolhouse, George Kurunus crowns himself King of the May, much as did Quasimodo. And Quella, one of the May Day Royal Princesses, sees George and notes that during the surreptitious act he is crying. She at last perceives his humanity and unhappiness. In the end, when all the handsome and conforming students reenter the building, all "the lean ball-players, the agile jitterbuggers, the leaping perch of yell-leaders, the golden-tongued winners of the declamation contests, Princes and Princesses, Duchesses and Kings," at least simpleminded Quella knows one more thing than the rest. The artist must crown himself in this world, must "create his own glory, in the face of opposition and conformity. The grasshopper's burden is that he must be considered a plague rather than a useful part of life."

VII   "Children of Old Somebody"

"Children of Old Somebody" is the first of three difficult stories which conclude the volume. Ostensibly it is the tale of a child disowned by his elderly parents and left at first to grow up in a log. Later the child is removed, but too late: already it is unfit to live in society, having grown up amongst wild things. The sin committed against this child is our own heritage and ancestry, Goyen seems to be saying. The disowned son roams the world, knocking on every door, to remind us of our sins. Indeed, Goyen titled the story not "Child of Old Somebody," but "Children of Old Somebody," enlarging the implications and refering to us all. The innocent figure roaming the world and knocking on doors and asking for our repentence surely is a Christ figure as well, reminding us of the famous painting of Christ at the door by the Pre-Raphaelite Holman Hunt. Christlike, the babe in the log represents perfect innocence. As Goyen tells us, "There was no hostility between its world and creatures' world, that hostility is learnt."

The babe in the log is also a Childe Percival figure. Indeed, Goyen's story relates to a special phenomenology of the child archetype, that of the abandonment of the child. Abandonment, exposure, and danger are all elaborations of the child's insignificant beginnings (in Christ's case, in a manger) and of its mysterious and miraculous birth (in Goyen's child's case, not an immaculate conception, but a conception between elderly parents). The child is a symbolic content, manifestly separated from its background (the mother), but sometimes including the mother in its perilous situation (as when she comes to nurse it). In Jungian terms, the child would be that third thing of an irrational nature which the unconscious psyche creates during a collision of opposites: "The new configuration is a nascent whole; it is on the way to wholeness, at least in so far as it excels in 'wholeness' the conscious mind when torn by opposites and surpasses it in completeness. For this reason all uniting symbols have a redemptive significance."[6]

And redemption is clearly Goyen's theme here. The "child" of the story is a symbol of the self's evolution toward independence. In order to achieve this, it must detach itself from its origins. Abandonment is therefore a necessary condition, and not just a concomitant symptom. The conflict is not to be overcome by the conscious mind's remaining caught between the opposites, and for this very reason it needs a symbol to point out the necessity of detaching itself from its origins. As Jung says of the psychic situation, "Because the symbol of the 'child' fascinates and grips the conscious mind, its redemptive effect passes over into consciousness and brings about that separation from the conflict-situation which the conscious mind by itself was unable to achieve."[7] The symbol anticipates a nascent state of consciousness: so long as it is not actually in being, the "child" remains a mythological projection, and one requiring renewal by ritual. As the Bible says, unless ye become as little children, you cannot enter the Kingdom of Heaven.

Goyen's baby here is as isolated in its environment as was Boy in *The House of Breath* and Son in "Pore Perrie." And all three, the baby, Boy, and Son, must detach themselves to achieve true selfhood. Consciously or unconsciously, Goyen in "Children of Old Somebody" has hit upon a timeless, archetypal situation. The fact that the child is delivered helpless unto the dangers of nature, but is endowed with superior powers to pull through, represents the strongest and most ineluctable urge in every being, namely, the urge to realize itself. The archetype of the child expresses man's wholeness. Jung has said it best: "The 'child' is all that is abandoned and exposed and at the same time divinely powerful; the insignificant, dubious beginning, and the triumphal end. The 'eternal child' in man is an indescribable experience, an incongruity, a handicap, and a divine prerogative; an imponderable that determines the ultimate worth or worthlessness of a personality."[8]

VIII   *"Nests in a Stone Image"*

"Nests in a Stone Image" consists of one man's ruminations in a hotel room on the eve of Easter. The hotel, like the highschool in "The Grasshopper's Burden," is stony and skull-like. The man's flesh and vulnerability are contrasted sharply with the coldness and permanence of the building and city in which they are situated. He sees himself perched like a bird in the stone mouth of some stone image.

During the course of the story all manner of human connections—social, spiritual, sexual—are overheard by him in the hotel. Only he seems to be alone. Yet by story's end we see that he is alone by choice, having renounced someone younger than himself, someone he loved but would rather abandon than see corrupted by their difference in age (and, possibly, their sameness of sex).

This suggestion that the renounced beloved might be of the same sex arises from the scene in which the protagonist is made love to by a woman, and finds himself unable to respond and, even, is unmanned. That the story occurs on Easter Eve and is resolved on Easter morning is perhaps meant to be significant: the impotent member shall rise, with glory, again.

IX *"A Shape of Light"*

The final story in the book, "A Shape of Light," ostensibly is the story of one Boney Benson, who lost both his wife and his unborn child, and consequently disfigured himself in guilt and expiation, burying his dismembered organ in the same grave as his loved ones. Thereafter his unborn child rose like a light to haunt him, a ghostly gesture of the inexpressible. As a total, the story is a meditation on the quest for the unanswerable, the unnamable, the unseen.

Boney's name of course indicates his mortality, and his seeking after the shape of light he sees in the dark is a Grail quest. He is a wise man following a strange star, that "gentle and curious light" which is no ordinary fireball or lantern, but a source of light which consequently becomes a source of spiritual strength. To become illumined is to become aware: As Goyen writes,

This radiant object shed the most delicate and pure clear illumination on little things in its path and along both sides, so that what it showed us who followed was the smallest detail of the world, the frail eternal life of the ground, the whiskers of a fieldmouse, the linked bones in the jointed feet of a hidden sleeping bird, a clean still white tincture of dew hanging like a fallen star on a blade of grass, a hairy worm on a stem like one lost eyebrow, the hued crescent of the shade of a sloughed snake like a small pale fallen rainbow. . . .

Clearly, to follow the light is to be in greater communion with the things of this earth. To follow the light is to follow Christ. ("I am the light and the way." "I am the resurrection and the light.") To follow the light is to follow the spirit. Thus, Boney's unread message, which he sends heavenward on a kite (". . . send up a message!"), is the emblem of our need to communicate with that power beyond us all. And though the kite falls, becomes, like Boney, a mere skeleton, the message sails on. Through Goyen's story, the lost message is risen and reclaimed "and fixed forever in the light of so much darkness and of so many meanings."

As in "Children of Old Somebody," Goyen here works with archetypal material. As pointed out, in Christianity Jesus was a light shining in the dark. As Jung says of Jesus, "Whether he lit the light with his own strength, or whether he was the victim of the universal longing for light and broke down under it, are questions which, for lack of reliable information, only faith can decide."[9] In another tradition, within the Tibetan Book of the Great Liberation, we read that those "fettered by desires cannot perceive the Clear Light." Here the clear light refers to the One Mind. Boney's withdrawing from the conscious world is a quest for the healing power.

In most of the numerous forms of mysticism, in fact, the central mystical experience of enlightenment is appropriately symbolized by light. And, as Jung says, "It is a curious paradox that the approach to a region which seems to us the way into utter darkness should yield the light of illumination as its fruit. . . . Many initiation ceremonies stage a descent into the cave, a diving down into the depths of the baptismal waters, or a return to the womb of rebirth. Rebirth symbolism simply describes the union of opposites—conscious and unconscious—by means of concretistic analogies. Underlying all rebirth symbolism is the transcendent function. Since this function results in an increase of consciousness (the previous condition augmented by the addition of formerly unconscious contents), the new condition carries more insight, which is symbolised by more light. It is therefore a more enlightened state compared with the relative darkness of the previous state. In many cases the light even appears in the form of a vision."[10] This would seem to be the case with Goyen's Boney Benson.

In addition, there is even an historical precedent for Goyen's light-seeking hermit, an actual person he may or may not have read about. I refer to the visions of the Blessed Brother Klaus. In 1947 Nicholas of Flüe, called "Bruder Klaus," was canonized by Pope Pius XII and declared the patron saint of Switzerland. During his lifetime (1417–1487), he abandoned his wife and children to live in a hermitage in Unterwalden. The single most significant event in Nicholas's life was the apparition of light, of surpassing intensity, in the form of a human face. The oldest extant account of Nicholas's life is a biography by Heinrich Wolflin (b. 1470), who wrote:

All who came to him were filled with terror at the first glance. As to the cause of this, he himself used to say that he had seen a piercing light resembling a human face. At the sight of it he feared that his heart would burst into little pieces. Overcome with terror, he instantly turned his face away and fell to the ground. And that was the reason why his face was now terrible to others.[11]

Goyen's Boney Benson is a modern Nicholas, a real spiritual anchorite with a singular inner life, a life for which no merely natural grounds can be adduced. In his unearthly quest, he is a figure central to a moving and disturbing book.

CHAPTER 4

In a Farther Country

I *The Romance of Prophecy*

A prophet, as the saying goes, is not known in his own country. So it has been with William Goyen. Certainly Goyen's prophetic second novel, *In a Farther Country* (1955), is not known here as well as it should be. Indeed, it is out of print in the United States, while continuing to sell in English, French, and German editions. The long second chapter, "The Roadrunner in Woolworth's," was reprinted in *Selected Writings of William Goyen* (1974), and that is all of it currently available. Yet the book is not only one of Goyen's most significant, but also a highly relevant document, published years ahead of its time, examining in those pre-Rachel Carson years such environmental and ecological problems as air-and-water pollution and the extinction of numerous species. For that reason, if for no other (and there are numerous others), this book should be read in our time—when each day is greeted by reports of yet another species about to vanish from earth: the last peregrine falcon, the last blue whale, the all-but-last tiger.

The book, while not so complex as *The House of Breath*, is still not easily summarized. Its heroine is Marietta McGee-Chavez, who is of mixed heritage (Irish and Spanish) and who lives on West 23rd Street in New York City. She longs for her homeland of the mesas and valleys and mountains of New Mexico. She is one of the last to sew the ancient Colcha stitch, an embroidery stitch handed down for centuries by Spanish women. In the din and dirtiness of New York City, Marietta honors and yearns for her homeland through the creation of an old and delicate art. Her husband, Thomas Harold McGee, runs a shop below their dwelling. It is called "Artifices of Spain" and here he sells reproductions and facsimiles of genuine classic Spanish art. Marietta, a halfbreed, lives between the honest art above and imitations of it below. The subtle theme of the novel is threaded on this duality and the conflict within it.

In the pet department of a nearby Woolworth's Marietta finds a faded, languishing bird. She is certain that the bird is a roadrunner, a noble and charming and vanishing symbol of her race. The pet department people tell her that the bird is a macaw. The manager allows Marietta to come and sit with the bird at night when Woolworth's is dark and empty, to keep him company and to bring back to him something of his own old country. The macaw dies, however, and Marietta and the manager mourn him. Later, when the bird miraculously revives, the manager brings the bird to Marietta's apartment, where there begins a dreaming-back of the enchanted country of New Mexico, which Marietta thinks she sees in the autumn colors of the bird's breast. These are the same colors and of the same texture as the fading woven hanging (from which the vision of the novel has risen).

The novel now develops through the succession of several visitors—wanderers, questing persons, lost persons—who come upon the visionary dwelling in the New Mexico land where Marietta and Thomas McGee live. The episodes are magical, lyrical, comic. Each arriving person tells a tale of his history, an adventure of pain and beauty which is revealed for the first time, never told before. (In this sense the structure of the book is not unlike that of Michael Bennett's Broadway production *A Chorus Line*, which was hailed as so original in the mid 1970s.) In Goyen's romance the ambience, the environment created by Marietta for these apocalyptic moments in the lives of these seeking and now-sharing people, is called "Spain"—a "farther" country.

The final paragraph of the novel, the coda, sets down the source and image of the novel. It tells of an embroidered curtain that hangs in a

falling house of mud and straw in the far Southwest of America. Upon it, in a wilderness of thread, are the entangled and half-vanished figures of men and women under a raveling sky, and standing before them is the haunting shape of a bird. . . . Because of the great age of the hanging, constructed of just unlashing thread in an ancient stitch, the thread has faded into colors of earth and fallen to the texture of withered grass, as if nature had made it and left it there. And were drawing it back again.

And this artifice was wrought by the dream that passes over that vanishing company, scattering into wilderness of brambles and seed.

At the time of publication the book was received with incomprehension if not indifference. Part of the reason Goyen's message
fell on deaf ears was, perhaps, a matter of technique. He treated
these problems, his themes, not in a naturalistic or realistic manner
at all. Goyen did not aspire to become the Upton Sinclair of the
ecological or the urban crisis. Instead, he attacked the problems
within the elusive framework of a romance, and as such the book is
designated by a subtitle. (The first novel, *The House of Breath*, was
also very much a romance rather than a novel, but was less quixotic
in its integration of imagination, memory, and perception. For a
fascinating study of the real and the unreal in that book, see the
remarks by Gaston Bachelard in his *The Poetics of Space* [1964].)

In a Farther Country is a romance in the sense that Hawthorne
defined one; and since there is evidence that that author's works
have had a powerful influence upon Goyen, Hawthorne's definition
is worth quoting:

When a writer calls his work a Romance, it need hardly be observed that he
wishes to claim a certain latitude, both as to its fashion and material, which
he would not have felt himself entitled to assume had he professed to be
writing a Novel. The latter form of composition is presumed to aim at a very
minute fidelity, not merely to the possible, but to the probable and ordinary
course of man's experience. The former . . . has fairly a right to present
that truth under circumstances, to a great extent, of the writer's own
choosing or creation . . . .

Hawthorne called for restraint in the use of these liberties, especially cautioning one "to mingle the Marvelous rather as a slight,
delicate, and evanescent flavor, than as any portion of the actual
substance of the dish offered to the public." It is in degree rather
than in spirit that Goyen exceeded Hawthorne. His conception of
the romance—with two resurrections in one story!—is more marvelous than real. But both *In a Farther Country* and Hawthorne's
The House of the Seven Gables can be seen as romances in what
Hawthorne calls the "attempt to connect a bygone time with the
very present that is flitting away from us."

The romantic genre was a propitious choice for Goyen, allowing
the poetic writer a freedom of time and place and movement unknown in the realistic novel. His central characters, all people who
are displaced in milieu and spirit, can freely shuttle back and forth
in time and place, imagining themselves to be where they are not.

Once the heroine, one Marietta McGee-Chavez, acquires the totem "road runner" for herself (in reality a faded-out macaw), she dreams herself out of her city apartment and into an adobe house on the plains. Most of the book's action occurs within the field of her dream. The book bears no more resemblance to the usual novel than, say, Virginia Woolf's *Orlando,* and in this respect typifies those qualities quoted in Chapter Two as remarked by Anais Nin in *The Novel of the Future.*

The last two paragraphs, which form a coda to the book, reveal that all the characters and actions which preceded were dream-products of the heroine, mere imaginative projections from an embroidered curtain upon which the lifeless prototypes had been stitched.

The frailty of the flesh, of the thread, and of the ancient art of the Colcha stitch from which the curtain was created, are all recurring motifs in the romance. The tapestry which contains them and into which Marietta enters is like the looking-glass through which Lewis Carroll's Alice passes. It is significant that Goyen, in the very last sentence, raises the additional possibility that, instead of the company having been dreamed by the heroine, the curtain itself was dreamed by the company. This is quite like Carroll's Alice asking, in the last chapter of *Through the Looking-glass,* who it was who dreamed it all. She knew it must have been either herself or the Red King. And she was pretty sure it was herself. But since she was, after all, a part of his dream, and he a part of hers, she could not be certain who dreamed it. Carroll's Alice and Goyen's Marietta share this and other uncertainties revolving about the unreality of the real, and Goyen would agree with the lines from Carroll's poem which form the coda to the looking-glass adventure: "Ever drifting down the steam—/ lingering in the golden gleam—/ Life, what is it but a dream?"

This romantic conception has been misunderstood and has led through the years to some highly inaccurate interpretations of *In a Farther Country.* Frederick J. Hoffman, one of Goyen's more sympathetic critics, is at first confused by it, writing in *The Art of Southern Fiction,* "The novel begins in New York City. (It may also remain there, or it may never really have ventured east of some place in New Mexico.)" Later, in the same discussion, Hoffman is totally wrong, assuming "the setting is apparently shifted soon to the Southwest."[1]

Marietta's Southwest in the romance is but a Southwest of the mind. Displaced and unhappy, a victim of what Saul Bellow once called "deep city vexation," she nevertheless must remain in the city, and therefore begins in her unhappiness to move in a field which is almost exclusively mental. (Another Goyen character, Princis Lester of the latter novella, "A Tale of Inheritence," suffers the same delusions.) Marietta's room, with its fire-escape bars at the window, is described several times as a cage, and she recognizes in the caged macaw in Woolworth's a similar displaced spirit. She mentally translates the macaw into a roadrunner because "Marietta McGee-Chavez's father had considered the massacre of the road-runner an evil turn in the world and said it was the end of an old time and the beginning of a sad new one, and that a message to the world was destroyed in him, as if a letter or a will had been torn up in the wind and blown over the countryside."

The massacre of the roadrunner is but one slaughter prefigured in the book. One character vividly recalls seeing a sad menagerie, "showing what few native things are left in this country," which included, among others, "the last prairie chicken in the world." Further, Goyen shows we have isolated and exiled whole races; another character speaks of his dispossessed grandmother, with "the face of Spanish noblewomen under a Cities Service cap." And we have defiled the waters and the air; a third character searched for the pure Thousand and One Islands and found only one, and it was "beer-colored."

Like the roadrunner on the busy highways of the New West, himself a messenger of nature being killed by modern civilization, the macaw in Woolworth's is a wild thing out of his element. By extension, Marietta herself is a wild thing in the plastic world of Manhattan. Goyen uses Woolworth's synthetic surfaces and pro-cessed air as a microcosm of the modern world. It is significant that the Woolworth's pet department clerk sprays the scent of pine among the creatures' cages at night, and whistles bird calls over the sounds of the traffic, both attempts to counteract the artificial en-vironment.

That the times are out of joint and that things are at an end is also portrayed by Marietta's watch, which was her father's and which now she keeps in a plastic heart-shaped box. Significantly, it keeps no time: in the plastic world it is always nine o'clock in the heart. Nine traditionally is the symbolic number for terminations, being the triangle of the ternary and the triplication of the triple, therefore representing the end-limit of the numerical series before its return to unity—an observation Goyen may or may not consciously have acknowledged.[2]

The book's title, then, comes into focus when we acknowledge "the farther country" to be not Spain or New Mexico, and certainly not New York City, but rather, the farther reaches of the imagination, which can salvage the spirit in a bad time. One of the book's essential themes is the survival of the imagination in a world where imagination is dying—an insensitive world established in the very first paragraph, where the constant stream of trucks on West 23rd Street emblemizes the omnipresent threat of mechanization.

An earlier working title Goyen had given the book was *Surely the People Is Grass*.[3] With its biblical allusion to *I Peter*, that title underscores yet another of the book's messages: the people are grass in that they are ephemeral, green in a season and quickly withering. They are also grass in that they belong to, and are one with, the world of grass from which they feel wrenched when absent: "So men and women carry countries in them and, falling, the country in their breast falls in them," Goyen writes.

II *The Romance of Exile*

This romance, then, is about exiles—animals exiled from their natural habitat, but more especially human victims of the unnatural environment man has created. The present unnatural state of the world is presented most succinctly in the soliloquy of the Woolworth floorwalker:

Do you realize . . . that in all the walking I have done in Woolworth's, I could have got clear to Arizona by this time and breathed me some fresh air instead of talcum powder and hair oil with Lanolin and toothpaste with chlorophyll and fifty other things with something added? The world is taking a terrible turn, if you think about it—something is being added to everything. It will suddenly stop when somebody revolutionizes the industry by deciding to take everything out of something except what is there to start with. Then we will just have the simple thing again. For a little while we will have very brief labels; and then somebody will have to add something again.

Everyone in the romance is an exile torn between dualities, beginning with Marietta herself, who becomes a mother-confessor for all the other characters, the act of confession restoring order and sanity to the lives of the confessors. Marietta McGee-Chavez, as her name confirms, is possessed of a conflict of the blood: she is half pure Spanish, half pure Scots-Irish (perhaps suggesting, as Hoffman conjectures, that the spirit of romance is in conflict with the blood of the Calvinists). The name also suggests sexual dualities within Marietta. More important, however, she is essentially a country person whose spirit is dying in the city. Goyen clearly is saying that with the death of the spirit comes the death of art. Marietta is a true artist, but the art she practices is a dying one: she apparently is the last living carrier of the art of the Colcha stitch. Her art is the art of creating from thread. And, like thread, the spirit of art is fragile. We must guard against the extinction not only of God-given creatures and elements, but of God-given talents as well.

The other exiles suffering dual conflictions—all of whose personalities bear significance—are Mr. MacDougal, whose love of austere and classical art must yield to his craving for the more reckless things of Spain and who wishes to be an artist but can only copy; the clerk who must flee his noisy apartment house each evening to seek quiet among the pets of Woolworth's; Mr. Thwaite Cumberly, who as a child was punished for dancing and now is an adult disappointed in his lack of grace; Mr. Chalmers Egstrom, who killed his best friend on Highway 66; Oris, a displaced Englishwoman; Lois Fuchs, haunted by her dead twin as well as by her dead lover; Jack Flanders, a suicidal actor who is alien to his family and to the family of man; Father Trask and Sister Angelica, two spiritual souls in the world of the flesh; and Sabino, a lively little bullfighter now working as city coroner. Goyen portrays each with the greatest engagment and sympathy.

The theme of duality as portrayed in all these characters is ultimately extended symbolically to Marietta's dwelling as well: " 'Artifices of Spain,' being darkened by buildings on both sides, as well as the workshop on the second floor, needed artificial light all day. This gave it a ghastly cast as if underground. But Spain above was in a sunny space, looking free over the roofs of buildings. . . . "

Marietta's salon where, Sybillike, she receives these friends, is called Spain because she aspires to Spanishness—Spain being for her a legendary center of beauty and truth. In her fantasies she welcomes all these callers in her role as an agent for restoring love and beauty to an ugly world. The only unwelcome caller is Mr. MacDougal, who can enter the Spain of her mind only after he has qualified to do so by making something genuine and not imitative.

He does so in the beautiful sarcophagus he carves for Mr. Egstrom. Marietta's Spain is "a speaking place and a joining place, a community of happenings through which people in it can reach each other and through which they can come to love each other." In 1955 William Goyen was anticipating the love-ins and happenings of the late 1960s and early 1970s.

But this Spain is more, too. It is synonymous with the artistic imagination. At one point Goyen has his Marietta exclaim, "The uncertainty of Spain! It is such a delicate country. The least doubt of it can burn it away or sell it out." The delicacy of the creative process is implicit not only in the fragile threads of Marietta's art, already discussed, but in the strings of the marvelous (in Hawthorne's sense) mandolin, which are made of the finest human hair. Hair, like thread, is one of man's most ancient symbols, denoting the essential connection between any of the different planes on which he moves—the spiritual, the social, the biological, etc.[4]

The delicacy of the imagination, then, is ultimately linked with the power of love, for which the lover's mandolin is a potent totem. This link is amply demonstrated by the book's two "resurrections." The first is the revival of the faint macaw, who is given up for dead in the killing air of Woolworth's but who rises again with glory in Marietta's Spain. The second is the raising up of Chalmers Egstrom, for whom last rites have been performed. Given the proper love and the proper atmosphere, Goyen is saying, the dying can revive. The inhabitants of Marietta's Spain find they all have suffered alike from isolation and bifurcation. The "oneness" of their condition is made graphic by the dance they all perform, Fellini-fashion, and by the author's careful unity of symbols throughout. Just as all the characters come to understand and love one another, become in effect one body, so too they are shown to all be made of the same substance, the same "dust" of Spain. Michel Lucazean saw this when he wrote in 1963, "The rushes and seeds that serve for the decoration of the room and are attracted into the dream are matched with the burrs of Jack Flander's beard, the seeds of the castanets, the vegetable metamorphosis of Oris, and even the deep-sunken primeval seed-girdle of the fisherman."[5]

III *Awakening from the Dream*

At the conclusion Marietta awakens from her dream, only to see the words "MOVING AND STORAGE" on the flashing neon light across the way. The words are the book's final pronouncement on the instability of the world and human relations. Yet Marietta can now better cope with the world, because through her dreaming she has acknowledged some essential truths about herself and the world. (In this she differs greatly from Princis Lester, of "A Tale of Inheritence"; Princis loses herself totally in her dreams, whereas Marietta finds salvation). Like the physical trestle Marietta put across the dooryard, she now has built a spiritual bridge or trestle between herself and the world of moving and storage. The sensitive *can* prevail. Or, as Quixote discovers in Tennessee Williams's *Camino Real*, the violets can break the rocks.

As an artist figure, Marietta perhaps comes closest of all Goyen's characters to saying what the author personally feels about life and art. In the book he calls for a balance of nature, and at one point Lois Fuchs pontificates, "Human nature troubles the purity of nature." But Marietta elsewhere takes a more liberal view and instructs us that "if you live a life of just people, something of nature in you will die; if there is no field where grass grows, you will die—you cannot root your life in people. If you live a life of just nature, all fields with nothing human passing through them or planting in them, you will die again." A careful balance must be struck between man and his environment.

That this balance is often unthinkingly destroyed by man is shown in Goyen's parable of the farmer who spares the giant snake (one of many giant snakes in Goyen's fiction—there are others in "Rhody's Path" and *Come, the Restorer* and *The Diamond Rattler*). Sparing the serpent, the farmer later rejoices to find that the snake had been sent to help him by destroying pestilential insects: "Too often we persecute our salvation, which has journeyed a long hard way to get to us, we kill it on its way to us, through fear or lack of waiting to see."

Man has killed off species before taking the time to study their value or to perceive the consequences. He has not taken things in their season, which is the great lesson of *In a Farther Country*. Toward the conclusion, in one of the most beautiful passages William Goyen has given us anywhere, the author makes a plea, in purest poetry, that we not force the world into an unnatural state:

Let yourself sink down to the root of yourself, do not hold it back! Get off the top of the earth in your wintertime! Dead leaves don't mean death. But no, we force ourselves to stay on the surface, policing the landscape, searching searching for a spring flowering when it is winter; as though a tree were to hang false leaves about itself all winter long and play summer. Whom would it fool? Not even the birds, who know green leaf from *papier maché*. We have forgotten how to *wait*, to let happen in season; we *force;* and so we violate. We cannot wait to let happen, we say, else we shall be destroyed; it feels too *late:* we have set this false weather and cycle of season into motion and we must keep it going. But alas, we must wait, as we must breathe, else we die.

What more vital message could there be for us today than this, found in Goyen's "romance" of over two decades ago?

CHAPTER 5

The Faces of Blood Kindred

I *Three Modes*

SUBTITLED "A Novella and Ten Stories," *The Faces of Blood Kindred*, Goyen's second collection of short fiction, is more obviously a collection than was the highly unified *Ghost and Flesh*. *The Faces of Blood Kindred* in some ways seems for Goyen a transitional book, with three distinctly different modes contained within its covers.

There is, first, the novella, "A Tale of Inheritance" (retitled "Zamour" in the German edition, and later in Goyen's own *Collected Stories*). This long narrative seems to belong with Goyen's more outrageous earlier visions, such as "The White Rooster"; surely the mad and drowning bearded Princis Lester could well be a sister of Little Pigeon in "The Letter in the Cedarchest."

A second mode is that of nondramatic musings in stories which barely seem to move forward in time or place. Rather than creating fictional characters and having them tell their tales, in these Goyen seems intent upon elaborating upon some intensely personal symbols which he calls (in "The Moss Rose") "eternal images"—a moth, a flower, a dead horse—and relating, through the third-person narrative rather than the first-person, their significance to his own life. One would expect that the shift from the first-person narrative form of *Ghost and Flesh* to these third-person pieces would provide greater aesthetic distance from his material. Such is not the case. These later stories are, by and large, intensely personal and philosophical outpourings rather than dramatizations.

The third strain evidenced is an element previously undeveloped in Goyen, that of overt humor. The opening story, "Savata, My Fair Sister," provides a liberal dosage of that. It is the piece which opened up the comic genre for Goyen, and provided the inspiration for his next book, the novel *The Fair Sister* (based upon "Savata, My Fair Sister"), as well as the screamingly funny story "Tapioca Surprise" and the Mr. de Persia sections of the novel *Come, the Restorer*.

II *Savata*

"Savata, My Fair Sister" is an apparently light-hearted dance upon the claims of flesh and soul, mind and heart, word and deed. It concerns two sisters, Savata and Ruby Drew, who are described as "black Jews"—members of not just one minority, but two, whose common bonds should have united them. Yet Savata's fairer skin sets her apart even from her sister, just as surely as does Princis Lester's lack of a beard set her apart from the bearded sisters in the novella which follows. One also recalls in this same volume the crippled foot of the grandfather in "Old Wildwood" and the harelip of the cousin James in the title story. Indeed the book is full of people whose physical differences are signs of their spiritual nonconformities. In all these stories Goyen muses on alienation and personal dissociation from one's surroundings. None is more an outcast than the fair-complected Savata. Her sister attempts to console her with the observation that her differentness is a blessing rather than a curse, that the Lord has set her aside, marking her for special work. But Savata will at first have none of that.

She rebels against her inheritance, and begins to use her looks and talent to serve the flesh rather than the spirit, becoming "a revue singer" and a nightclub entertainer. But Ruby Drew finally convinces her to abandon that career in favor of working for the Lord. Together Ruby Drew and Savata establish the Light of the World Holiness Church in Brooklyn. Savata is ordained its bishop, and Ruby Drew becomes the church business manager. All goes well until Canaan Johnson appears on the scene. An anti-Christ, he turns Savata's head back toward materialism. The spirituality of the fair sister is lost.

The story concludes with Canaan Johnson revealing his duplicitous ways by stealing from the church and disappearing. As penance, Savata humbles herself and becomes a housekeeper, simultaneously on her hands and knees to the Lord and doing practical labor.

Goyen tells this tale with great humor and gusto. It is the first overtly humorous of his writings, contrasting greatly with the seriousness of *The House of Breath* and *Ghost and Flesh*. On the other hand, he does run the risk of appearing patronizing to his black sisters, of perpetuating certain racial stereotypes. These risks are usually avoided, however, and the story successfully communicates Goyen's themes of the problems of communal heredity and the quest for personal identity in a lighter, but still effective, manner.

III   "The Faces of Blood Kindred"

The title story, and the second in the volume, also explores the indebtedness of blood relative to blood relative. "The Faces of Blood Kindred" continues to explore this haunting question of ancestry and personal identity, "a particle of answer in the face of the world," that which is inherited and which marks us more completely than any external trappings.

Basically the story revolves around two scenes. In the first, a country boy betrays his city cousin by accidentally killing his fighting cock by casting a stone upon it: the cock had been eating the boy's grandmother's figs, and he had merely meant to stop it. It is a highly symbolic scene, functioning much in the manner of the killing of the white rooster in "The White Rooster," with the timid cousin's destruction of the lusty cornish cock symbolic of his desire to extinguish all that is instinctual and dangerous. Further, the boy James identifies with the cock. When the cousin kills it, something in James also dies. (James's identification with the cock parallels the grandfather's identification with the fowl in "The White Rooster," and the boy's with the coyote in "The Thief Coyote.")

The second scene occurs years later. The cousin does not see James until then, when the cousin, successful, is being honored in a large midwestern city. James approaches the cousin, clearly hoping to talk, to atone, but someone pulls him around, with his back to James, to congratulate him upon his honor. When the cousin finally turns around again, James is gone. The protagonist seems akin to St. Peter, who denied Christ more than once. And like Peter, he agonizes over his own duplicity, somehow intertwined with memories of a crowing cock. The cousin's glance of outrage "struck like a blow against ancestral countenance, had left a scar of resemblance, ancient and unchanging through the generations, on the faces of the grandmother, of the aunts, the cousins, his own father, and his father's father; and would mark his own face longer than the stamp of any stranger's honor that would change nothing."

IV *"Old Wildwood"*

When William Goyen went through his entire body of work to make selections for inclusion in his *Selected Writings of William Goyen* (1974), "Old Wildwood" was one of only two stories he reprinted from *The Faces of Blood Kindred*. And it is one of the remarkable things from the second collection. Another memory piece, really a poem of sorts, it is the reveries of a narrator (clearly Goyen himself) while ensconced in the ancient stone city of Rome and reflecting upon his real heritage—one not of stone at all, but of wood: the timber tracks which have long been cleared, the wildwoods which now are thinned and tamed.

The incident which triggers the narrator's memory is the receipt of a letter informing him of his grandfather's death. The shock sets memory into play, and one particular evening especially is remembered, an evening when the grandfather (obviously the same grandfather who appears in other Goyen stories), brings a woman back to the cabin he is sharing with the young grandson, and proceeds to make love to her, thinking the boy asleep. In the sexual performance on the adjacent cot the boy perceives, precociously, the history of the race and of human frailty. It was at once disastrous and beautiful. In the act even the grandfather's deformed foot, the cloven hoof of deviltry and carnality, of Pan himself, "had a very special beauty and grace of movement, a lovely secret performance hidden in it that had seemed a shame on his person and a flaw upon the rock. It had something, even, of a bird's movements in it. It was the crooked foot that was the source and the meaning of the strange and lovely and somehow delicate disaster on the bed. . . ."

From this shape and movement, the narrator has made a special memory for his own. It finally assumes the shape of an author's creed for William Goyen! In that secret performance Goyen perceives the whole history of everything, especially of everything which is ephemeral like the disappearing wildwoods of the world, and he therefore resolves to do,

in his time, some work to bring about through an enduring rock-silence a secret performance with something, some rock-force, some tide-force, some lovely, hearty, fine wildwood wildwater thing always living in him through his ancestry and now brought to sense in him, that old gamy wilderness bequeathed him; how shaggy-headed, crooked-footed perfection would be what he would work for, some marvelous, reckless and imperfect loveliness, proclaiming about the ways of men in the world and all that befell them, all that glorified, all that damned them, clearing and covering over and clearing again, on and on and on . . . .

It is a marvelous description of the very aims and effects of William Goyen's own life work, a body of fiction which depicts not the deadness and coldness and permanence of stone, but rather the life and warmth and ultimate perishability of wood.

V   "The Moss Rose"

"The Moss Rose" is a common Texas flower which the author, in New York City, later observes on Third Avenue, where he finds it is called "portulaca." While called different names, it basically is the same star-shaped flower bringing joy to common people. By any other name, it would be for Goyen a symbol of timelessness and changelessness, the subjects of the story.

Actually the story manages to encompass many symbols of change and permanence. The demolished Third Avenue elevated and the Texas train rails; the iron fire escape and the portulaca; the gray in the author's hair and the unchanging youthfulness of his memory of Jessy. (The sister Jessy seems the same who appears and dies in *The House of Breath*.) The author combines these symbols to brood on the nature of changing elements: "By a certain time something, some structure, in every life is gone, and becomes a memory. But it has caused something: a change, an attitude, an aspect. It is the effect of what was, he thought, going on, that is the long-lastingness in us."

And later the author thinks/writes:

The same patterns do exist all over the world, in cities and towns, wherever people live and arrange life around themselves. . . . And a sudden sight of this human pattern in one place restores a lost recognition of it in another, far away, through an eternal image of a simple flower, in the hands and care of both; and in a moment's illumination there was in him the certain knowledge of unity forever working to stitch and tie, like a quilt, the human world into a simple shape of repetition and variation of what seems a meaningless and haphazard design whose whole was hostile to its parts and seemed set on disordering them.

VI   "The Armadillo Basket"

The Starnes Family, of *The House of Breath*, are revisited in "The

Armadillo Basket." The story involves two progressive sisters, Lucy and Mary, and their old-fashioned sister, Laura, who lives in the past. In their conflict they remind us of Savata pitted against her old-fashioned sister Ruby Drew, or the city of Houston commenting on the backward ways of Princis Lester.

On the day of the story, the three sisters are to visit the family plot in the cemetery. Yet at the last moment Laura will not go, because her mother's picture has fallen from the wall, an act she interprets as an omen of bad luck. The other two think her silly and superstitious. Yet, upon their return, they find she has died. So was there not something to the omen after all? Laura had greatly resembled her mother. Moreover, the mother had possessed an armadillo basket. Then, when visiting the family grave plot, a real armadillo had sat upon the mother's grave. Isn't there, then, some unseen spirit controlling all of these things?

"Never know who's next," Mary declares at one point. Indeed we don't. But at least signs can help us, Goyen says, a message repeated many times in *Ghost and Flesh*.

VII   *"Rhody's Path"*

"Rhody's Path" is a typical Goyen story. Many of the author's favorite properties are here—the small-town girl run away to the city (called Rhody, but obviously the selfsame Sue Emma Starnes of *The House of Breath*); the escaped rattlesnake (who reappears in *Come, the Restorer*, as well as in the play, *The Diamond Rattler*); the flagpole sitter (of "Figure Over the Town"); the faith healer (of *Come, the Restorer* and the play *A Possibility of Oil*), etc. It is almost like Fellini's film *8½*, in which he orders all the people and objects from his life to parade and dance upon the screen.

The snake, chained to earth, and the flagpole sitter, braving the air, are two symbols of salvation in the story. The pasture in this story, as in *The House of Breath*, functions as the gateway to the world. Yet Rhody's path, through it and out of it and beyond it, is the path less traveled by. She is nonconformist and worldly. Yet her actual life is saved during the story's course by a simple, homemade remedy: country hog lard. The Reverend Peters, with his sensual name and joined, hairy eyebrows, proves to be less effective in saving a life than a good old country remedy. Knowing this, he departs (only to reappear in *Come, the Restorer*). Home could be Rhody's salvation and redemption, the city her corruption and error. Yet like so many of the characters in both books of stories, Rhody is of the restless breed. She cannot stay put in one place, but must eternally shuffle in between two worlds, belonging to neither.

VIII   *"A People of Grass"*

A wonderful story, "A People of Grass" combines the May Fete of "The Grasshopper's Burden" with the imperfect sister Jessy of "The Moss Rose" and *The House of Breath*, revealing again how Goyen remines the same material and can discover yet more gold. Chosen by Goyen as the second story to represent *The Faces of Blood Kindred* in his *Selected Writings*, it begins with an adult's fleeting glimpse of little Italian girls adorned with flowers, a glimpse which triggers his memory of an early revelation—the May Day ceremony in which his sister, in a homemade flower costume, trips and falls over one of her own skirt petals. A seemingly trivial incident, it nevertheless revealed to the narrator a galaxy of human frailties. He was descended, surely, from "a people of grass," from seed that grows but is perishable and highly fallible. His mother's hands were flawed, could not create a perfect dress; his sister was imperfect, could not rise without tripping; his father felt inadequate and underprivileged; and even the narrator, cast as "King of the Flowers," could not bring his sister or his family to flower. His magic wand is, after all, mere cardboard.

Yet, in the later May Pole dance, his sister is surely the most accomplished of them all. Even her early failure touches her then with some magic and dedication to overcome. From mistake and deprivation can come achievement, Goyen says. But even that achievement is transitory: all is as ephemeral as the winds of May. Goyen's symbols, especially the disembodied crepe-paper petal on the grass, perfectly communicate his intentions.

IX   *"Zamour"*

"A Tale of Inheritance" (titled "Zamour" in the *Collected Stories*) seems to me one of Goyen's finest stories, though critics are hardly in agreement. William Peden, for instance, finds the tale "both impressive and irritating. It is marred by an overelaborate concern for language and technique at the expense of clarity of vision."[1] Yet the message seems clear enough. While Goyen clearly deplores the loss of tradition and the change of the landscape due to "progress," he is also capable of seeing that too great a resistance to change can in itself be dangerous. When Princis Lester refuses to adapt to the city ways of Houston, preferring instead to become a recluse in her own house, she degenerates into insanity.

In the beginning Princis was just that, one of the princesses of this world, privileged by beauty. Her sisters, on the other hand, were armed as eccentrics by the possession of little black beards. Princis feels alienated from them, and accepts an offer of marriage and a move to the city of Houston. But she is no more at home there than is Marietta McGee-Chavez at home in New York City, in *In a Farther Country*. As one of the neighbors says of Princis Lester Simpson, "Whenever I get homesick for Red River County, which is less and less—it's all so changed, not a bit like it used to be there—I just go look in Mrs. Simpson's house and feel I've been home to Red River County right on Hines Street in Houston. Why does she harbor home and past?"

Princis harbors home and past because, in a changing world, she is the last of the little country women. It is in her blood to hold out. She even holds out against her new husband, refusing to consummate their marriage, in a symbolic refusal to embrace new ways.

Alone in an alien world, Princis becomes increasingly paranoid. "The neighborhood is trying to keep the pension from us," she tells her cat, Zamour, at one point. And later, when the roof begins to leak, "They are trying to flood us out, before the pension comes." Finally, when a hurricane occurs, "They are tearing our house down and turning the Gulf of Mexico upon our heads." Eventually, in her madness, the flood in her hurricaned house becomes the Red River.

Princis's real legacy is not the railroad pension of her late husband, but rather the beard of her two sisters. There is a central paradox at work here: at first she came to feel the outsider because she does not have a beard, yet her sisters are comfortable banded together because both are bearded. Only when Princis's chin also sprouts a beard, as an outward sign of her inner acceptance of her ancestry, her link of flesh and blood and kindredness, does she become a whole person. It is not enough to maintain Red River roots; blood runs thicker than water, and the blood of kinship must be acknowledged. The true red river is blood. Eventually Princis even renounces her beloved Zamour, who was, after all, a foundling cat and a stranger, in favor of sisterhood. The family becomes the norm for her, not the world, and even that which is freaky in familihood must be acknowledged.

"A Tale of Inheritance" paves the way for much of the message and characterization of the later novel *Come, the Restorer*. The little bearded Lester sisters, for instance, playing the xylophone together, have their counterparts in the later novel. And Wylie Prescott's rise to fortune and his mansion—imported, piece by piece from France—is elaborated upon in *Come, the Restorer*.

X   *"The Geranium"*

Princis Lester's degeneration is counterpointed by "The Geranium," a tale of renewal and regeneration, in which a couple have come through a long hard winter with their marriage scarcely surviving. The husband feels there is no physical contact between him and his life, let alone spiritual contact. But, like the symbolic geranium plant of the title, man has an infinite capacity for renewal. The blood-red plant clearly is a regenerative, even a sexual symbol: "For she saw, deep in the shadowy crevice between two limbs of the geranium, a cluster of little hairy pods gathered round together and covered with a frail green membrane. . . ."

The geranium agrees with Goyen's philosophy that everything has its season, everyone his time: "Slowly and ever so patiently, through a long, blossomless time, the geranium had waited by the window; and now it showed upon its body the sign of the changes that had happened within itself."

It is a philosophy Goyen expounds to greater length in the novel *In a Farther Country*. In its pursuit of the instinctual, the story relates to Goyen's "The Thief Coyote" and to much of D. H. Lawrence.

XI   *"The Horse and the Day Moth"*

In "The Horse and the Day Moth," two seemingly disparate events in the writer's life give rise to philosophical speculations on "the relationships between objects seen, now and then, between moments and sights, disparate and antithetical as they seemed."

The story is "about" the necessity for awaiting connections, to perceive, patiently, how all things work together toward some ultimate meaning. In this sense, it is related to "The Geranium." On the other hand, it is a story of losses as well as gains. The horse fallen dead represents large losses, public and for all the world to see. The moth stain on the fingers is a tiny gain, private and known only to the gainer. Yet both relate to the dream of the loss of the mother.

With the horse as a physical symbol, and the moth as a spiritual one, Goyen is uniting the one world with the other, and acknowledging the necessity for both.

XII "*There Are Ravens to Feed Us*"

The protagonist of the final story, "There Are Ravens to Feed Us," seems the same tormented soul encountered in the hotel room in "Nests in a Stone Image" (from *Ghost and Flesh*). In the midst of his anguish he encounters a moving scene of human beauty as significant as the little girls of Rome and the disastrous Texas May Day Fete, in "A People of Grass." For in this story, out of a house of hate springs a beautiful vision, and that beauty is the redemption of all darkness and grief.

The vision of the wedding party, in their pastels and their carrying of flowers, is akin to the products of the artist's imagination. After all his wrestling and torment, Goyen seems to be saying, the difficult and seemingly impossible miracle of creativity occurs. When it does, it is always a new beginning, an occasion for hope and betterment.

CHAPTER 6

The Fair Sister

I *Savata Rides Again*

WHEN Goyen's third novel, *The Fair Sister*,[1] appeared in 1963, eight years after the second, even his most sympathetic readers must have been surprised, for it differs greatly from most of the work which preceded it.

It is firmly set in Philadelphia and Brooklyn, not the Southwest. (*In a Farther Country* is physically set in Manhattan, but the field of action is nearly always the "Spain" of the Southwest and of the heroine's imagination.) The entire cast of *The Fair Sister* consists of blacks, not whites. It is highly farcical rather than intensely serious. And it reads at times like the book for a splendid, big-budget Broadway musical.

The novel was written at the suggestion of Goyen's editor, Sam Vaughan, of Doubleday, who saw the possibility for a larger work growing out of Goyen's earlier story, "Savata, My Fair Sister" from *The Faces of Blood Kindred.* The plot goes something like this:

Ruby Drew, a large and unattractive black woman connected with the Church Zealous in Philadelphia, has a beautiful and fair-com-plected sister named Savata. At an early age Savata becomes prodigal and wild, running away to sing and dance in St. Louis nightclubs. Ruby Drew gets on a train to retrieve Savata and restore her to the North. Watching her sister's nightclub act through a keyhole, Ruby Drew feels she is experiencing her true calling:

Ruby Drew, 'tis meet and right that you came here, bidding your hunches, and following the Lord's goading. For your greatest challenge (and oh my God my greatest toil, I can tell you) is materialized right here before you, through a keyhole and hunching in feathers and sparkles. 'Twas that fiery moment of revelation like some saints had, St. Augustine and some of those women saints. . . ."

Ruby accepts the challenge, and manages to convince Savata to return to Philadelphia to lend her talents to the Church Zealous and to Prince o'Light, its prettily handsome leader. Savata becomes a trainee, a recruit for bishop of the church. She does, that is, until she runs away, to be found in a bar by Prince o'Light and Ruby Drew, who get her to return once more.

Savata continues her journey toward a bishopric, learning Hebrew and practicing sermons on all subjects. She receives her preaching papers, finally, in an extravagant ceremony "that the angels in Heaven would have wept at. . . . It made *Aida* look like a summer-camp show." Afterwards Bishop Savata and Ruby Drew move to Brooklyn, to establish the Light of the World Holiness Church, for which Savata appoints Ruby Drew business manager.

Bishop Savata sings and preaches on the sidewalks, to draw crowds (mostly male) into the church. The church is soon prospering. Though Savata leaves the Light of the World Church building essentially as she found it, she does take on a personal secretary and begins being driven in a limousine. She becomes, in fact, a Superstar. While Ruby Drew does not approve of Savata's ways, she feels she can control the situation. That is, until the devil incarnate appears to upset things. He appears in the form of a "teacher" by the name of Canaan Johnson.

William Goyen once said his personal choice for the role of Canaan Johnson, if the book were ever produced on stage or film, was Sammy Davis, Jr.[2] And Mr. Davis does possess the electricity, the wicked humor, the wiliness, to convey the complexity and duplicity of Canaan Johnson's character. As the negative, evil force counteracting Ruby Drew's positive, good influence, he is a powerful figure in the novel, so powerful that when Goyen was faced with the task of choosing but one section from the novel for inclusion in his *Selected Writings*, he chose the chapter introducing Canaan Johnson.

The moment Canaan Johnson appears, relations between Ruby Drew and her fair sister begin to degenerate. Savata falls totally under his influence, deposes Ruby Drew as church business manager, appointing Canaan Johnson instead. He begins to alter the church to his own image, of course—spending $3,000 for a pipe organ, $600 for a piano, and always encouraging Savata to own more material possessions. She acquires, among other things, a Persian lamb coat and a diamond cluster pin. She also starts to dye her hair red. Ruby Drew lectures her on the necessity of reforming her ways, and on the perfidy of Canaan's character:

"You are the fair one," I said, "and you are marked off to do a special service by Jesus, and you are just having the wool pulled over your eyes by this studying man. He is smart, I grant you that, and knows Hebrew and studies up all day in his room; but he is studying up, at your expense, to leave you in the end; and pocket all your earnings in his pocket."

Ruby Drew begs to be reinstated as business manager. Savata refuses.

Afterwards Ruby Drew accidentally encounters a talented boy evangelist, Cubsy Hall. She sees Cubsy Hall as the instrument of her reinstatement and her vengeance as well. Together Cubsy and Savata would be a born duo—"a team worth a million"—for the church. There would be no further need for the likes of Mr. Canaan Johnson.

But the necessary deal is not consummated with Cubsy's manager, and even a phone call that results in the sudden appearance of Prince o'Light does not produce Canaan's voluntary removal. Savata shamelessly disavows her loyalty to Prince o'Light and confirms allegiance to Canaan Johnson. In the words of Ruby Drew, "She betrayed the great man who had brought her to her glory and she turned him out like a traitor. Oh what a terrible moment it was! It had all come to this."

Ruby Drew decides to demand an open hearing—to bring the conflict before the entire congregation. The hearing develops into a trial, and the trial scene, in Chapter Thirteen, is the high point of the novel, not merely in terms of dramatic development, but also for its outrageous hilarity. Throughout the novel, Ruby Drew has been acquiring new words for her vocabulary by sparring with the scholarly Canaan Johnson. In the trial, she finally attempts to use all his own words against him. More often than not, she misuses them, and rather than clarifying issues, she obfuscates them, as when she claims her rival has "ensconced" the church members, and that the church itself had become an "androgyne that is neither fish nor fowl." And so forth. Whenever Ruby Drew finds her audience's attention flagging, she throws in some totally unrelated phrases about "the Seven Assassins of Palumbo" riding onward, a story she once heard Canaan Johnson tell and which had been, at the time, spellbinding.

Ruby Drew loses the trial, of course, and Canaan Johnson keeps his job—until, that is, he takes his leave one day, without warning, taking with him the church funds and Savata's diamond cluster pin. (She had cedar-closeted the fur coat, but moths demolished that. Savata is quickly instructed in the vanity of earthly possessions.)

Afterward, Savata takes over Ruby Drew's housecleaning jobs, as penance, and Prince o'Light returns to ordain Ruby Drew the Bishop of Light of the World Holiness Church (in a very simple ceremony which contrasts greatly with Savata's). Yet Ruby Drew is unable to build up the church thereafter. The glory has gone out of her preaching. When Savata herself finally disappears again, true to character, Ruby Drew no longer has the will to pursue her. After all, "We would just have the whole thing over again. No. I let her go." And so the short novel ends.

II *The Conflict between Body and Soul*

One could argue that, within the fabric of this story, are the threads of all of Goyen's best fiction. It is, to begin with, an introspective narrative by a seeker. Secondly, there is the duality between Savata and Ruby Drew, that essential physical disparity between them which causes spiritual alienation. Savata's light skin makes of her as much an outcast from her family as does Princis Lester's lack of beard (in *A Tale of Inheritance*) or Folner's homosexuality (in *The House of Breath*).

In many ways, Savata is much like Folner. Both run away from home at an early age to join show business. Both travel with a trunkful of showy dresses and boa feathers. Savata is but a Folner of a different color, a Folner of a different sex. And as with so many of Goyen's characters, she is a displaced person. Instead of being a country soul forced to live in the city, like Marietta Chavez-McGee and Princis Lester, she is a show-business personality forced to perform within the confines of the church. Also, as Louise Gossett already has observed, the battle in this novel is no longer between the self and the outside world ruined by machination (as in *In a Farther Country* and, to a lesser extent, *The House of Breath*). Rather, it is a conflict between the body and the soul, "neither sufficient by itself to make a complete human being."[3]

And whereas the struggle between good and evil, light and dark, sin and pleasure, has been central to Goyen's work from the beginning, *The Fair Sister* marks a decided change in the author's attitude, particularly toward sex. The intense guilt over masturbation and fornication in *The House of Breath* has segued into wry amusement and satire. Prince o'Light's incipient homosexuality and Savata's liberal carnality, for instance, are subjects for good humor rather than exacerbation. It is an attitude Goyen is to continue and expand upon in the highly sexual, highly comic *Come, the Restorer*—the novel which in fact follows chronologically in the Goyen canon, and the title of which is itself a sexual pun.

There is yet another way in which *The Fair Sister*, a seemingly funny and frivolous novel, is absolutely typical of the best of Goyen, a novelist noted for his seriousness. That is in its dramatization of a quintessential Goyen theme, that of the poor, the ugly, or the disinherited who has a much greater sensitivity to beauty and yet cannot possess it. Ruby Drew can no more hold Savata than Pore Perrie can keep Son, or Malley Ganchion can keep Berryben.[4] In *The Fair Sister* this theme is realized in the beautiful and lamentable scene in the fourth chapter, when Ruby Drew, in a wistful moment, is left alone with all Savata's gorgeous and showy things:

Needing a little magic, I flung over the cover and opened the trunk. Mine eyes was dazzled by green and purple feathers, shining bands and colored shoes, and especially one beautiful cloak of red and purple with some white fur stuff on it. I took the cloak out. I put it around my shoulders. It was a little big for me, long to the floor, but it was pretty. It made me feel—different. I strode around in it before the mirror. Attractive.

Then the "glory demon" gets hold of Ruby Drew, and she puts on ornament after ornament and begins to perform a savage dance. Rather than David's joyful dance before the Ark, it is a parody of Savata's sinful bump and grind. At the climax of Ruby Drew's dance, the door opens and her spectacle is viewed by Savata herself. Nowhere else in the novel is the disparity between these sisters so apparent, so pitiable. While the crux of the novel remains Ruby Drew's inability to remake Savata into her own spiritual image, it is also apparent that one fact of her own personality desires to remake her dumpy self into the physical image of Savata, an impossible desire.

One of the glories of this novel is Ruby Drew's infatuation with words. Goyen builds double entendre upon double entendre as Ruby Drew misunderstands words she thinks she knows, as when

Cubsy Hall apostrophizes Savata as "some fable Priestess of Eros, some houri. . . ." Ruby Drew immediately jumps in:

"What's that word houri?" I asked.
"Look it up, Ruby," castigated Canaan Johnson.
"I don't like the sound of it," I objected.
"Look it up and don't distract Cubsy Hall's beautiful elegy to Savata."
"Elegy?" I says. "What's that?"

The novel is named after Savata, but ultimately it is Ruby Drew who draws our attention and sympathies. As Joseph L. Blotner concludes in his essay on the novel,

Ruby Drew lacks the beauty, the fire, the flair of her fair sister, but William Goyen shows us through her words and thoughts that the treasures she has piled up—drudging in ramshackle churches, weeping on the crosstown bus—are richer than those of words alone.[5]

CHAPTER 7

A Book of Jesus

I Relationship to the Fiction

IF the high comedy and slickness of *The Fair Sister* surprised some of Goyen's admirers, *A Book of Jesus* (1973), coming after ten years of silence, must have been even more surprising. It was, to begin with, Goyen's first nonfiction book. Also, it was a deliberately "inspirational" work, dealing with Christ's promise of abiding love and personal fulfillment, an attempt to retell the story of Jesus in the simplest kind of language, to reveal the man not only through his teachings and sayings but also through his relationships with others. The dust jacket informs us that Goyen "wrote *A Book of Jesus* because he was compelled to, and his view of Jesus has the power of personal discovery."

And so it does. Goyen's affinity for Jesus should not be surprising. For, as Goyen inscribed in this writer's personal copy of the book in April, 1973, "He was on the flagpole and He was with the white rooster and He helped Swimma Starnes pack her suitcase for the hundredth time." In a very real sense, Goyen has been writing the story of Jesus all his life. One need only think of the many resurrections in his work, from that of the white rooster to that of Chalmers Egstrom in *In a Farther Country:*

Marietta cried out, "Everybody! The object of the wake is laughing alive in the doorway to Spain!" and Chalmers Egstrom laughed out, "Do not dig my grave!" and laughed more.

"Forget the dead man and celebrate the live!" Marietta called.[1]

Like the egg which his last name connotes, Egstrom is a sign of potentiality, of seed, of generation, of the mystery of life.

Moreover, as I stated at the conclusion of Chapter Six of this book, Goyen has been occupied in most of his fiction with the struggle between good and evil, the conflicts between the soul and the body, the ghost and the flesh. Berryben and Christy in *The House of Breath*, the nephew James in *The Faces of Blood Kindred*, and Addis Adair of *Come, the Restorer* are all potential Christ figures—all, in Goyen's own words, "figures of sleep, death, resurrection, beauty, and power."[2]

Addis Adair, hero of the novel Goyen was to write almost immediately after *A Book of Jesus*, is especially Christlike. He was, to begin with, of miraculous birth, "since it was obvious to all and known by a few who passed it on, that his mother was a virgin; said he had special powers, said he was a wonder child, a holy child."[3] Later Addis-Christ leaves his parents and draws large crowds all over the land through his "miraculous" feats of walking on a clothesline, defying the laws of gravity almost as if walking on water. He becomes baptized, is later mocked and stoned, ultimately betrayed, later hunted down, and symbolically is hanged in a tree! The Christly parallels, however unintentional on Goyen's part, seem undeniably present.[4]

Goyen's nonfictional life of Jesus, then, should not come as a surprise, though some readers might wonder why a talented novelist such as Goyen would spend time writing yet another life of Jesus, when there have been so many such "lives" already. We can assume that Goyen did not make the attempt with any hopes of imparting new information about the Man whose dimly viewed life splits the history of the world, since, indeed, Goyen is no scholar. Almost all the background for his book comes directly from the four Gospels of the New Testament, works accessible to all. Goyen did not even take advantage of additional accounts in Josephus, the Apocrypha, the Book of Enoch, or the new materials from the Dead Sea Scrolls. Rather, Goyen's intention seems to be not to inform, but to inspire—to impart subjective rather than objective truths. This occurs when Goyen retells the familiar facts and communicates them poetically and subjectively. In this sense his book joins that handful of weightier studies of Christ by creative writers rather than scholars and theologians, books such as François Mauriac's *Life of Jesus* (1937) and Robert Graves's *King Jesus* (1946). It is because of Goyen's special gifts as an intuitive and at times mystical writer than one would wish to read this account of Jesus from His baptism to crucifixion.

II *A Physical Jesus*

Within the brief 143-page span, Goyen employs his considerable fictive powers to make Jesus of the Gospels a real and an individual being (as opposed to that artificial and composite one of so many theological studies). Goyen's Christ is an especially *physical* one who strides across the pages with energy and power:

This man Jesus was a man on earth, a man of flesh as well as spirit. He knew how flesh hurts. He touched, with his hands, *physical* humanity. . . ; he handled the flawed bodies of thousands. Jesus loved the physical . . . world and the suffering creature in man. He was so much a part of the substance of nature that it was the very material of his teaching (a grain of wheat, a mustard seed, a fruit tree that withers, is barren, or produces bad fruit; the grass that is like flesh that the wind blows over and withers). The man of the spirit honored the flesh which, though it die, must be straightened if it is bowed over, made sound if it is unsound, made clean if it is fouled with disease, by restoring and mending. He did it with his own hands and often with his own spittle. He loved the humanity of flesh that he touched, embraced, handled. He was a great gentle Nurse, soother of flesh as well as comforter of spirit. His physical embrace of humanity was a grand enveloping caress, a lifting up in his arms of the collapsed and fallen, a flesh-and-bone support for the stumbling, a warm broad human breast for the fainting head of the weak. (pp. 89–90)[5]

Goyen was quite aware of the extraordinarily physical—almost sensual—nature of his Jesus. In a letter to this writer, composed just at the completion of the composition of *A Book of Jesus* (December 2, 1970, Goyen wrote:

It's a swift, striking (as in a blow), physical little thing, this book; quite gracefully rude, like some farm instrument to be used by hand, a sickle or a hoe; and my Jesus snorts and sighs and groans, curses, spits, sticks his fingers in the ears of deaf people; and he *handles* mortality, touches the flesh of hundreds, heals that way. The experience of writing it has been an extraordinary experience. My discoveries were so exciting, so personal, sometimes, sometimes as ecstatic as few things I've known. . . .

Another compelling, original, and conceivably controversial aspect of Goyen's portrait is his conviction that Jesus' ministry was no benevolent crusade, but a radical and anarchical drive by an insurrectionist. Thus, Goyen's Jesus is a fugitive, like so many of his fictional characters. And this Jesus was not just fugitive in the last weeks of his life, but throughout the better part of it:

In reality, when we think about it, the greater part of his work was rarely done in a peaceful atmosphere. He had to work under pressure, against hecklers and rabble-rousers and spies. He had always been needled by smart questioners who wanted to make him angry, sharply challenged by other clever men who were no fools. In other words, this man's work was not at all a lovely sitting in a circle of sweet groves. It was done in peril, and swiftly, up and down the countryside, on roads and atop hills, in little villages for a while—but not for too long—in town churches, by the lake, in boats on the lake. In the smaller villages he was harassed on every turn. His life was a chase, and it swiftly became a deadly pursuit. (pp. 28–29)

As is evident from these several quotations, Goyen narrates the story in straightforward, King Jamesian language, making no conscious attempts to draw parallels with today's times and events (though the parallels are there to be drawn, verily). No hippie or Superstar, his Jesus is a hunted and marked man kept from his fullness, much like Christy/Christ of *The House of Breath*, hunting and hunted in the woods around Charity.

Goyen also reminds us, in *A Book of Jesus*, that Jesus was not only a great peacemaker, but also a great speechmaker. Goyen labels the parables of Jesus as "spare and explosive in their tightly-wound little bombs of truth." The book concludes, then, with a mini-anthology of "Words of Jesus" in an attempt to reveal the quality of His mind and His way of talking with people. As Goyen says in the "Author's Note" which begins the book, "The material preaches itself. I have hoped, simply, to try to tell again the story of the man, His world, His times, the people around Him."

Goyen realizes his modest ambitions. As a book in the Goyen canon, *A Book of Jesus* is perhaps the least important. But, as the Bible says, the last shall enter first. Perhaps this little book, so readable, so accessible, will lead others to Goyen's more complex and "creative" works. Further, as an exercise which broke a ten-year writer's block, and which led the author straightway into an allegorical novel which can compare favorably with anything he had previously written, *A Book of Jesus* was worth the doing. Let those who encounter Goyen for the first time through this nonfiction book go on to discover the riches of his fiction.

CHAPTER 8

Come, the Restorer

I A Crazy-Quilt Plot

GOYEN'S fourth novel and eighth book is a brief (180 pages) but immensely concentrated effort. Its themes, among others, are ecology, erection, and resurrection. In it he parades forth again, almost Fellinilike, a line of fantastic characters, each of whose eccentricities of body or spirit gives point to some facet of Goyen's message. In order to compare it to any other recent artistic creation, one must evoke Fellini's *Amarcord*, rather than any other novel. (Indeed, Fellini is said to have expressed great interest in Goyen's fiction in the past.) The novel combines Goyen's sense of place, displayed so richly in *The House of Breath*, with his generous sense of humor, earlier exhibited in *The Fair Sister*. The novel also extends his deep concern over ecology, explored earlier in *In a Farther Country*, and draws more fully upon the dream world of fantasy for its expression. In all these ways, *Come, the Restorer* represents a culmination in William Goyen's fiction.

The plot is a crazy one. Like all Goyen's novels, this one is hard to summarize. The plot spins off in several directions at once. Early in the book we are presented with the character of Mr. de Persia, the repairman, a great, impotent "maker" of things. Shortly thereafter he lies in a swoonlike sleep, resting in an enormous glass bathtub of his own making. Curiously, only his phallus (which never rose in life) is alert. It remains mightily erect for all to see. Mr. de Persia becomes a tourist attraction and a fertility figure around whom many legends and fantasies of birth, prosperity, and hope develop.

One night Mr. de Persia's body is stolen. After much conjecture and mystery, the body-snatchers are revealed to be a gypsy girl and two young boys. They have managed to spirit the body away in a hot-air balloon. Straddling Mr. de Persia's ever-ready sex, the girl

89

manages to get herself pregnant with his seed. Then the trio dispense with his sleeping body. Some say they saw the body of Mr. de Persia sailing through the air, rejected from the basket of the balloon. The body is never recovered.

But the body of Mr. de Persia's child is! The boy-child born of the gypsy girl is later abandoned by her, left in a hollow log. On his thigh is a birthmark in the shape of a harp. The baby is found by Jewell Adair, the frigid wife of Ace Adair. She raises him as her own, giving the child the name Addis. Addis Adair and his search for meaning in this life are central to the remainder of the novel. As Erika Duncan has written, "*Come, the Restorer* is the story of the orphan within all of us which must wander and go its own way, for in our deepest areas of being we are no human's child."[1]

As an adolescent Addis Adair leaves his foster mother and begins a graillike quest. He takes with him only a photograph of his dead foster father (Ace Adair having killed himself apparently over sexual deprivation), and a piece of his foster mother's old clothesline. Going from town to town, Addis stretches the clothesline between trees and learns to walk it. He becomes an aerialist. In the act of rope-walking he asserts his essential identity, finds his element. In time he becomes "an attraction." Many people follow him from town to town, but in time he loses his following and becomes a solitary.

Years pass. Addis becomes much transformed physically during his spiritual quest. Jewell Adair, in her wild grief over Ace's suicide and Addis's departure, also becomes much transformed. Here we must make a willful suspension of disbelief; for Goyen asks us to believe that when the two next meet in the great thicket, foster mother and adopted son do not recognize one another. Overcoming her frigidity at last, Jewel makes love to Addis. For the first time she comprehends the depths of her own passions. In passages of some of the most sexual (and most beautiful) writing in recent fiction, Goyen describes their unions in the woods.

What follows sounds like melodrama. Addis Adair accidentally hangs himself from a tree, like the biblical Absalom. It is only when Jewel finds him and thinks she is burying her young lover that she sees the harp-shaped birthmark and realizes she is burying her son as well. Only then does the incestuous nature of their affair occur to her. Then she, too, hangs herself from a tree. Yet a third party comes forward to attempt to save her. It is Mr. de Persia, alive all these years and wandering like the Wandering Jew. He sees Jewel's body and climbs up the tree in a fatal attempt to rescue her. Fatal because he too slips, falls, and is hanged.

The focus of the novel then shifts to Addis's real mother, the gypsy girl, who is discovered to be the wife of Fire Devil Prescott in the novel's last third. She lives in a mansion with a once-splendid circus horse, a creature who has now been castrated and who has lost his golden teeth and golden hooves. As if the hanging of Addis and Jewel and Mr. de Persia were not enough, Goyen then has the old horse hang itself, too: "a possible suicide . . . in his old swan-dive shape, shoes lustreless, mouth slack and gray, his head nevertheless held in its old arabesque as regal as in the olden days."[2]

On the basis of this plot summary, the novel sounds absurd. Yet as Erika Duncan concludes,

With the characters of this strange tale we have traveled many strenuous miles through realms of intermingling fantasy and reality, through folk tales, myth, and recreation of a pained and changing South. Yet we too have come out changed, startled and broken, as each primal image recurs, as each character is re-united in an altered way with those important personages of an incestuously complicated past, we feel "made whole," repaired, somehow, and ready to await the *new* of our life which existentially demands the dying of the old with the same courageous regality that the gypsy's beloved horse showed in its death. We feel a sense of their growth and resurrection as in the end we watch the faithful rattler Jake (the snake of the Oil King revivalist), "cast his fading rubies among the cool fronds and lie like a lamb of pure white among the lace and feathers and curling hair of pale and deep green fern. It was a breath-taking sight—the once-accurst dweller in the drought of the ground redeemed and transfigured in the living green."[3]

II *Novel of the Elements*

"Few people know—and they cannot tell—what went into the making of one rich American city," the book begins, in a narrative related by one soul who indeed remembers and is willing to share his recollections of the earlier days of the city of Rose, Texas. The early Rose was all its name implies—a town small, lovely, unspoiled, aggreeable to the eye and nose, the few prickles worth the beauty. It was a town which resembles in many ways Charity, of which Goyen wrote so eloquently in *The House of Breath*. The narration in the first section of *Come, the Restorer* gives us the lost Rose, not only the visible one which has become, due to greed and mismanagement, unlovely, spoiled, disagreeable to the senses. The narrator tells individual tales of some of the figures who made the town the city it is today, those "figures of sleep, death, resurrection, beauty, and power who were the ancestors and forebears of Rose" (p. x).

The story of Rose parallels the story of our national ecological travesty. Early in the narration we are given a potent symbol for the ruin of natural beauty Goyen laments. He writes of a nest of birds housed in an air-conditioning unit which are chopped to shreds when the machine is turned on. Nothing, Goyen seems to say, can condition the air as sweetly or naturally as that choir of birds we brutally have destroyed through mechanization and artificiality. Consciously or unconsciously, Goyen has created in the novel a major character for each of the four elements we have disturbed: earth, air, water, and fire.

Earth is the element of Oil King, formerly known as Cleon Peters, a snake preacher and healer. Unable to realize a Second Coming and unable to attain the Promised Land, he kneels instead to the given land beneath his very feet, becomes dirty in doing so, and discovers oil rather than salvation. He is like Peter, the Rock of the New Testament, turning to mud. Peter/Cleon Peters anoints his own head with oil, proclaims himself Oil King, and begins to preach a Gospel of Good News of Oil Glory.

Oil King's totem creature, the diamond-backed rattlesnake Jake, is of course also closely related to the earth, the one creature condemned to crawl closest to it. (Oil King and Jake are very much like the pair described in Goyen's earlier story, "Rhody's Path.") And at first the possibility of oil was a promise of good fortune to that part of Texas. As one character says to another, "We didn't do a thang . . . Lord put it in the ground, Oil King took it out. Now we're rich. Please don't trod on my zinnias" (p. 95).

Yet the promise of financial rewards created greater problems than it solved. Led by Wylie Prescott, that generation became a poisoned generation that ate its own poison, that cemented over good land and grass to create acres of cement slab. In short, it became a generation of greed and vulgarity who destroyed the common environment for private gain.

Prescott is Goyen's figure for the second element, fire. Labeled

"Firedevil Prescott," early in life he was a fighter of fires of the boomtown oilwells. Prescott is a satanic figure, deliberately depicted as the Devil incarnate. Sexually impotent—one of many characters so afflicted in the novel—he seems to receive a vicarious pleasure through entering the body of fires "as if it was just a lighted room where he was going to sit down and have him some supper or visit with somebody, not holding back, carrying a big red bottle, sausage-shaped, and out of which came foaming white stuff upon the flames, to quell them" (p. 148). The sexual connotations of Prescott's extinguisher and actions are obvious.

Just as Prescott goes to the very heart of fire and kills it, later he goes to the heart of the burnt-out timberland and kills it as well, first drilling it for oil, sending orange flame flashing in the air like a holocaust. Later he ruins the land by "developing" it. He "cut down green faster than a plague of locusts" (p. 155). Prescott was one of those men accursed with the gift of destruction:

He took away from Nature its pure self, its forces, and did not put back anything, but he added fake stuff—chemicals, preservatives, coloratives. His factories murdered rivers, spoiled freshness, soured and embittered sweetness, withered green. He was the first, the leader, the beginning of the generation that poisoned itself, that spoiled its own, that ate its own poison. Wylie Prescott left a ghost forest of burnouts, sinks from salt-water overflow, slews from oilwell drillings, junk from pipeline digging. Nothing lived in his devastation. He drilled and dug and hacked and tore up the wilderness. He opened out of the earth volcanoes of salt water that spewed hundreds of feet into the air, shot off geyers of salt and slag and crude that blackened trees and vines and encrusted acre upon acre with salt cake. He created a landscape of slews and sumps. (pp. 156–57)

Goyen gives us, by contrast, the strange and beautiful and creative character, Addis Adair. As the last three letters of his last name signify, his element is air. He is an Ariel figure who walks an aerial wire. Addis is most himself when walking a tightwire high in the air, usually strung between two limbs of a tall tree. If Goyen portrays Prescott as the Devil, as he surely does, Addis is (like Christy in *The House of Breath*) a Christ figure. Found in a log like a mythical baby of the tale "Children of Old Somebody," we are told of Addis:

The town spoke of him as one who had a Virgin Mother and was a son without a father (and spoke of his adopted father, Ace, as a man who had a virgin wife.) And a superstition developed about Addis Adair, as happens in towns, that said he was of miraculous birth, since it was obvious to all and known by a few who passed it on, that his mother was a virgin, said he had special powers, said he was a wonderchild, a holy child. . . . (p. 59)

At many points in telling the story of Addis Adair, Goyen seems to be rewriting his own *A Book of Jesus*. Addis even leaves his home as a boy, saying to his mother in Christlike elocution, "Woman what do you have to do with me?" Addis spends his life in a quest for his real father, the godlike Mr. de Persia. When Addis is not roaming the earth in search of the father, he is walking the wire, in his element, nearer to heaven than most mortals, walking the air as Jesus walked upon the water.

But man will not leave his earthly paradise alone. Addis is often threatened by the sound of explosions, of chainsaws, of "developers." The sinful encroachments of what passes for civilization come nearer daily. Addis cannot continue to survive, and in the end he is hanged from a tree, in a symbolic crucifixion, with only his mother at his feet to hear his last words, like Mary at the cross.

The last major character is Mr. de Persia himself, a man of salvations. He is the Restorer of the novel's title, the Redeemer for whose return so many wait. Yet, as Goyen also makes clear within the action of *In a Farther Country*, mere artifice cannot save the world, though it may be an individual's salvation. (In this respect, the content of Goyen's *Nine Poems* should also be examined; see the following chapter.)

Mr. de Persia is the god who fathers Addis, the holy son. It is he to whom the inhabitants of Rose turn to restore the glory which has passed away from this earth. Goyen brilliantly makes Mr. de Persia a restorer of fading photographs, of broken art objects, one who, in making small things whole, might restore the Whole. Mr. de Persia is a cynosure to whom the unwhole town turns, much as Carson McCullers's townspeople turned to her fictional and fabulous Antonopoulous in *The Heart Is a Lonely Hunter*. But neither the mute Antonopoulous nor the impotent Mr. de Persia can save a generation. His impotence is symbolic of an inability to function, despite the connotations of his name, de Persia—"of Persia"—from the land of art and artifice.

Later Mr. de Persia falls under a spell, and in his swoon becomes victim of Priapism, his eternally erect organ symbol of his fatherly state. In his condition he becomes the unconsummated bridgegroom of the entire town's imagination. Mr. de Persia's element apparently would be water, since he lies immobile in a special glass bathtub.

In his quest for his father, Addis's life is enjoined with that of Mr. de Persia. The Father and the Son become One, as Goyen prophesies: "Can somebody be both son and father?" (p. 87). Mr. de Persia also dies through hanging from a tree in a second symbolic crucifixion. (Goyen's mythical parallels seem to occur in doubles; recall the two resurrections in *In a Farther Country*.) His crucifixion comes after having been born again—a born-again Christian!—in the thicket, deprived of all memory of earlier times and thinking he was delivered in the thicket just as Addis was delivered and deposited in a hollow log: "They are both Christ figures and both are claimed by the wilderness. They need each other to exist, to form a whole. Their common and reciprocal story illustrates the revolving cycle of life."[4]

III   *Erection and Resurrection*

This novel, or rather, romance, of ups and downs, of power and impotence, is saturated with phallic imagery. It is as if Goyen's imagination somehow equates money power or spiritual power with sexual potency. When one is rich or in tune with the spiritual, one is literally "making it." At first there is Mr. de Persia, with his strange case of Priapism. Then there are his guards, power figures, who always awaken with erections. Then we are given Leander Suggins and Ace Adair, both suffering from unfulfilled sexual desires. Leander, we are told, would straddle anything with a hole, including a log! Finally, Ace's stepson, Addis, experiences an erection whenever he fulfills himself through walking the wire.

By contrast, the author also gives us a gallery of impotent men, notably Wylie Prescott, the younger Mr. de Persia, and the older Ace Adair.

There are, moreover, numerous symbolic or mythical male organs. These include the balloon in which Mr. de Persia is whisked away; Jake, the huge white rattlesnake who, at one time, seems the very source of Oil King's power—a power which he later transfers to Addis; the train engine, mighty machine on which the impotent Ace lashes himself; the oil rig on which Oil King rides up and down; the circus cannon which explodes and emasculates Horse, the fabulously endowed animal; Wylie Prescott's sausage-shaped fire extinguishers, mentioned earlier; the "immense organ of rubber" which is torn from the dummy of Mr. de Persia; the corn cob which is used to violate the body of Prescott's mistress (a detail recalling the rape of Temple Drake in Faulkner's *Sanctuary*); and the furiously gushing oilwells themselves, coming to violent and profitable climax. All these phallic fantasies lead one critic to proclaim, "The erection is probably the main character, the hero of this book, which tells us the good and bad fortunes, the ups and downs of the male organ."[5] This is misleading; the town of Rose itself is surely the main character of the chronicle. Nevertheless, the presence or lack of penile power is undeniably linked to the social, economic, and spiritual themes in the novel. Goyen himself grasps this, as when he writes, "In this world of quick fortunes one man went down and another rose up before you could tell what happened" (p. 114).

There has never before been a book by Goyen so permeated by sex. On the other hand, it must be stated that obviously sex has not been exploited to make the novel "sensational" and therefore "commercial." As Patrice Repusseau states, sex "is deeply rooted in the very fiber of the prose and serves many purposes. Actually, sex in general and the erection in particular are the blessed and, of course, demonic (everything being in everything) links that tie all the themes together, for the rises and the falls, like anything Goyen uses, are manifold, polysemic."[6] It is the only book by Goyen in which the word "come" in the title could be subject, as we have said, to sexual interpretation.

It is this mystical eroticism which distinguishes *Come, the Restorer* from other novels of new-found Texas oil money (such as Edna Ferber's *Giant* and Georgia McKinley's *Follow the Running Grass*). Given a theme which could encompass a massive chronicle, a book of Dickensian proportions, Goyen has instead created a tight, compressed, highly symbolic poem full of mystery, myth, and no small amount of humor. While *The Fair Sister* is oozing with wordplay and slapstick, *Come, the Restorer* is full of bawdry. Moreoever, the sex is of an extremely healthy, heterosexual kind. The chapter entitled "The Green Tree and the Dry" surely contains some of the most erotic love prose in print, written with the freedom D. H. Lawrence would exercise if he were alive in the 1970s. Indeed the only homosexuals in the novel are portrayed as figures of ridicule. This is a departure from the psychology of *The House of*

Breath, a novel in which unfulfilled homosexual longing seems at the heart of several protagonists' motivations.

Just as the tales in *Ghost and Flesh* show William Goyen's characters in search of what Jung calls an "individuation," those in *Come, the Restorer* seem to be totally immersed in the four elements in their quest for wholeness, understanding, and communication. As Boy says in Goyen's first novel, "I melted into the world and changed into everything that had ever been created or constructed . . . and everything entered into me, all involved in all."[7]

For its brevity, the novel is remarkably rich, entangled and clotted like the Great Thicket it portrays. The book's structure, nevertheless, could be improved. Conceived as a chronological saga, a chronicle, it devotes ten chapters to past Rose—the times of Mr. de Persia—and only four chapters to the era of Wylie Prescott (and these, alas, among the briefest), so that the novel has a curious imbalance. The reader longs for more about the Prescott era, especially about Selina Rosheen and her "Hidden Years." The book reads as though the author lost interest, after less than 200 pages, in rounding out the saga.

Come, the Restorer stands, despite this imbalance, as a highly original, indeed audacious, addition to the Goyen canon. It is, among other things, one of the few novels in which major characters are a snake, a horse, and the collective male penis. After this, one can only wonder where the imagination of William Goyen will go.

Nine Poems *and*
The Collected Stories

I *Exalted Times*

POETIC is one word often used to describe Goyen's work and world. In 1976 he published a small, beautiful book of nine poems which confirm the poetic roots of his prose. Written early in his career, before any of his books of fiction were published, the poems are built upon images of breath and blood, ghost and flesh, earth and fire and water—keys to the first novel which was to come, *The House of Breath*.

The book breaks into three sections of three poems each: "The Taos Poems," "Artifices of Blood and Breath," and "Three Artifices." The three Taos poems were written in El Prado in 1946; the first group of Artifices in Portland, during 1948–49; and the "Three Artifices," in Napa, California, during 1947. They come out of what Goyen calls "two exalted times" in his life:

"The first, the Taos poems, were written from my excitement over what was to be one of the deep influences on my life: Frieda Lawrence and life around her in El Prado, New Mexico. The second was the visionary experience of being in touch with the mysterious fountain of outpouring feeling (love, longing, homesickness, desire) that was generating my first novel, *The House of Breath*."[1]

Of the three groups, the three Taos poems are the most straightforward and literal, largely evocations of the living presence of Frieda Lawrence and the memory of D. H. Lawrence (1883–1930). The initial piece, titled simply "Frieda Lawrence," celebrates that strange, gentle woman as the embodiment of Lawrence's totem figure, the phoenix, that mythological bird of great beauty—one of a kind—fabled to live in the wilderness for countless years, finally to burn itself on a funeral pile and to rise from its own ashes in the freshness of youth and to live through another long cycle of years. The symbol fits Frieda, for, living long beyond her famous husband's death, she was Lawrence's emblem of immortality. A person of peerless excellence, she was a great figure and a paragon. Goyen saw her as having "the touch of greatness," "in spite of what they say." The "they" referred to here are the legions of sycophants and camp followers who streamed to Lawrence's home and later to his grave—petty figures when compared to Frieda. Goyen sees them as those "who only whirled around him, quarreling, / Like a flock of iridescent flies." The contrast between dirty, buzzing insects and the soaring, purifying phoenix is at the heart of the poem.

"Lawrence's Chapel at Kiowa" is a more complex composition. It recalls one fierce evening, the events of which Goyen takes to be archetypal. The ghost of Lawrence dominates all six stanzas—as ash in an urn, as imagined knocking at the chapel door ("like a drum"), as presence in a Lawrence painting ("the fierce Male / taking the Female to his thigh; / The room was aglow with a savage passion . . .").

The movement of the poem seems intentionally to parallel the progress of the sexual act, the act so central to Lawrence's work. The poem begins with a mood of gentleness, with "the untouchable desert / Flowing smooth as uncreased silk." Then the spirit is knocking and rapping at the entrance, the portal to experience. This leads to the climax, in the fourth and fifth stanzas, in which, like seducer and seduced, murderer and murdered, coyotes and wild creatures are "raucous under the night." The final stanza is all contentment and afterglow, the meaning of the act and the meaning of the poem one of love and celebration:

> And then everything went all gentle and sweet,
> A tender stir of wind was in the trees, a kind of ocean-wind;
>   there was a singing.
> And then the rapping from the direction of the chapel
> Was not at all a thing that wanted to be freed,
> But a caress, a drum-beat of praise and benediction,
> And it lulled us to sleep.[2]

Lawrence's ashes figure in a third poem, "The Hailstorm at Mabeltown," in which Lawrence in death is perceived as being in a state safer and greater than any of Goyen's living companions, who endure a dangerous hailstorm with him. Any one of these mortals could be extinguished utterly by a handful of hail against the temples. The hail, of course, is symbolic of all the elements of danger—danger which cannot touch Lawrence's ashes: "Ashes are more everlasting than fire."

Less mystical and more linear than "Lawrence's Chapel at Kiowa," this third Lawrence poem is distinguished by utterly fresh and striking imagery, including evocations of "the creased tents of trees," "the naked scalp of earth," "the hail coming down over the / Sacred Mountain like a herd of sheep / Or like rice thrown at a wedding," and "the acrid body / odor of the rain coming / Perfumed with the breath of sage and cedar." This is highly precise and economical poetry, worthy of the Imagists, with the exception that Goyen goes beyond mere Imagism to draw universal truths from his exquisite particulars.

The second group, "Artifices of Blood and Breath," are more metaphysical and less imagistic. In their thorny, alliterative language they resemble, somewhat, the poetry of Dylan Thomas, a poet who may or may not have been an influence upon Goyen at this stage of his career. The spirit of Thomas seems to be felt in lines such as "And betrayal double-backed in all the beds" and "While the hunch-and-slide worm movements on the worn floor / Hunch and slide over fruit and leaf."

These three poems are meditations upon existence and alienation, creation and destruction. In the first, "The Bird of Fire," the poet assumes a Stephen Dedalus-like stance: "O I who care will breathe an image into time with my / limitable breath /As the seasound is breathed forever within the shell." In an indifferent world, it is the poet who cares, and in his caring he can create a difference. Unless the poet lives up to his obligation to create, to breathe his own images into time, he is nothing more than an ornament in this world. Goyen clearly equates creation with love and wholeness, love which can break forth "like an unexpected bird of fire / To chime his fiery hour and tremble the clock." The clock here is Time itself, set akimbo by an act of timeless creation.

Indifference and inertia are not all the artist must overcome: "arteries of blooded terror lie wound within the works / of everything." Again, love and the love of creation can overcome. The created thing becomes as remote and distinct as the moon. The poem concludes with a stunning lunar image:

> O moon of frozen breath and smoke
> You are the serenest shape of violence blown clear
>   of violence, and safe,
> Into a ruinless iridescence of all meaning
>   and all peace,
> A bubble blown by a raving child.

The antipodes of Beast and Prince, Dionysiac and Apollonian, employed in this poem, are also at the heart of "The Wheel of Blood," a study of the war between the violent and the sublime. One is reminded here of Eliot's *Four Quartets*, especially the line "rat's feet over broken glass." Goyen's cry of distress reads,

> Alone and in our most ultimate distresses
> We wait for the crashing of glass
> When the glittering Redemption will come
> Springing corruptible from a ruin of shattered glass. . . .

"The Bridge of Breath" is Goyen's figure for life—that bridge between the two great silences, prebirth and postdeath. (It is a figure he later used in the story "Bridge of Music, River of Sand.") That thing which breaks the silences is communication, "the syntax of breath," "a curving sentence of stone." Weightless, invisible, light as breath, the human utterance can reach "From blue silence to blue silence through a pestilence of stars, / Murmuring the speech of stones." The poem is a third variation on Goyen's theme of the creation of order amidst malevolent disorder. Again it is the created thing, the Word, the artifact, the artifice, which saves with grace.

The collection concludes with "Three Artifices," poems given the physical shape of the paragraph of prose. Nevertheless they are truly poetic, especially the first, "Greets the Sea," which may well be the most striking piece in the book. It is a rather elaborate and extended metaphorical study of images for the sea itself, "wild and ruffling his huge uncurried body and lashing his great mane upon the sodden beach. He was flinging his tousled hair upon the beach, tossing it back, then flinging it forward upon the beach again. Shell and weed were tangled in his hair." The sea here is personified as a great shaggy being with human characteristics. In the poem's second stanza Goyen refers to his wartime experience in the navy, and then proceeds to write of the sea's many enchantments. He concludes with an original image for the waves: " . . . he sprayed out a glittering peacock tail of beaded spangles that shattered and fell upon a slime-green rock pied by guano of gulls. . . ." The sibilation and the alliteration of these lines recreate the sound as well as the look of the sea. The striking piece concludes with an observation of the indifference of the sea. Indifference is an attitude which concludes the remaining two Artifices as well—the indifference of the spider in his web and of the sea in his bed once more. The spider amidst his beautiful web is a figure for the destruction and terror which Goyen finds at the center of the universe. Conversely, the woman's red slipper sucked out to sea in the final poem is an image of a manmade, earthly thing which is overcome by unearthly, universal forces. Both are striking examples of Goyen's feeling for a world of give and take, birth and death, indifference and rare illumination.

II *New Stories: "Tenant in the Garden"*

In 1975 Goyen published his *Collected Stories*. The volume contained all the stories previously commented upon here, plus seven which had been uncollected. The uncollected work for the most part is vintage Goyen and a worthy conclusion to our considerations, especially "Figure Over the Town," "Bridge of Music, River of Sand," and "Tenant in the Garden."

A major affliction of our human condition, for Goyen, is a lack of firm footing in this world. Much of his work concerns the search for a place where one can be oneself—not a material position, but a spiritual one-ness with one's surroundings. This is the story of "Tenant in the Garden." It is a story which Erwin Helms may have had in mind when he introduced Goyen's four-tale volume, *Short Stories*, in which it first appeared.

Helms speaks of the author's work as pieces which "reveal him as a writer who reacts violently against the philistinism and the conformity of our time and tries to overcome them by rediscovering the poetic faculty of imagination. Deliberately he seems to accept the role of the outsider who tries to find singleness of mind in a distracted, dollar-chasing world. Isolated and lonely, he longs to reestablish human feeling, becoming a poet in search of an intact world, of a secure home."[3]

In the story, a little old printer, Mr. Stevens, comes to a small town in the Napa Valley, to teach printing in the junior high school. He is an artistic, frail type who has spent his life quietly and meagerly. After some difficulty securing housing, Mr. Stevens finds exactly the place where he wishes to live: a playhouse in the garden of a large, old-fashioned house. Its smallness makes him feel secure and warm and hidden. Its differentness—though Goyen does not say so, and his character does not think so within the story—is a badge of his difference from those surrounding him, of his artistic inclinations.

Mr. Stevens's inability to cope with the world at large is shown in his ineptness in handling his classes with any degree of peace or even safety. The boys roughhouse and chase one another. Mr. Stevens's voice is so small—the small, still voice of the artist in the vast world—that he cannot be heard above the din. That Goyen intends Mr. Stevens to be comprehended as the figure of the artist in society is undeniable: "Why had he taken this job that had cruelly brought him out into the open world where he seemed to cause strife and antagonism just by being the way he was? He was meant to sit quietly, some place, alone."[4]

For a while, the playhouse serves as his sanctuary. Then representatives from society come to badger him. At first boys come and proclaim, "We heard that you lived in a playhouse and came to see if we could believe our eyes . . ." (p. 220). When told the house was his house, they conclude, "He ought to be in the nut house." By choosing a way of life different from the norm, he is thought crazy—a typical reaction to the artist in many times.

Later other representatives come, among them the city commission, wanting to evict him because the house has no running water. By their standards, Mr. Stevens's house "does not meet the requirements of the city pertaining to dwellings" (p. 225). The language Goyen uses here is purposefully full of legalese. Proclaiming Mr. Stevens a misfit, the commission departs.

In its handling of the mistreatment of the artist in society, this story bears a resemblance to the author's "Figure Over the Town," which will be discussed shortly. It even more closely resembles John Updike's story "The Hermit," published years after the Goyen tale and perhaps influenced by it. But "Tenant in the Garden" continues beyond its indictment of communal conformity. At the conclusion, the little playhouse is being used as a gathering place by a number of citizens, for social purposes. While the artist must be apart, something in the majority of men urges them to come together. Neither condition is wrong, and both must be tolerated.

III *"The Thief Coyote"*

"The Thief Coyote" appeared in *Southwest Review* in 1971, and Goyen has written an unproduced screenplay based upon it. It clearly is a story of which he is fond. Like the majority of these later stories, it deals with one individual's necessity to escape a crude, captious community and to nurture his own fantasies. In this tale the coyote running wild in the valley is a symbol of the free spirit, the instinctual, the natural, as well as the struggle to survive. Its color—red—underscores these implications, being associated with blood, wounds, death-throes, sublimation, and passion. Throughout the writings of Jung (whom Goyen has read: see the *Interview* appended to this volume), the animal stands for the nonhuman psyche, for the world of subhuman instincts, and for the unconscious areas of the psyche. Goyen's young protagonist, Jim Coopers, and his identification with the coyote, conform with these readings while perhaps even confirming them. His initials and his early death qualify him as one of Goyen's Christ figures.

When news of the turkey-stealing coyote reaches the valley, some want to trap it, but the consensus wins. A group sets out to kill it—an act paralleling the stifling of the free and the instinctual in society: "A reward to the man who gets him" (p. 231). Young Jim Coopers clearly is the outsider here. He is a peacemaker. He refuses to take a pull on the whiskey bottle when it is ritualistically passed to him. He is more interested in eating nuts—natural food—than in killing the animal. He is, in the hunt, merely a conscripted follower, above their bloodlust and lewd storytelling: "He backed off a little from the others and sat in the shadow to himself, and from there he watched his own secret vision in the fire which the men's stories tried to shame" (p. 234).

His own secret vision! Again in a Goyen story we have a young visionary who perceives his artistic vocation. Jim is like Boy Ganchion of *The House of Breath.* He is the nonconformist, the boy who would rather pick pecans than kill hogs or brand cattle. His peers make fun of him. He alone among them is above thoughts of personal glory or increase. Like the artist, this gatherer of nuts would make the most of what was fully given. In the face of irrationality, "his real and loving work was to collect quietly what the earth had made and had fallen, yielded to him upon the ground, and store away a quiet gathering-up . . ." (p. 235).

The story has a tragic ending. Gone off, alone, to crack his pecans, Jim and his sounds are mistaken for the coyote itself. He is shot dead, the nonconformist Christ figure eliminated in an act of violence. Nevertheless, Goyen seems to say, the likes of Jim Coopers will continue. The instinctual and spiritual will somehow prevail. Even as the men bear back the boy's body, Lazamian sees, or thinks he sees, "the fleeting vision of a coyote leaping across the Coopers' field towards the pecan grove with a turkey in his mouth" (p. 239). Jim and the coyote are one figure, one spirit. In its symbology and theme, this is the most Laurentian of Goyen's stories.

IV *Two Chapters from* Half a Look of Cain

"The Enchanted Nurse" and "The Rescue" are parts of the same story—the story of a narrator named Curran, who is a hospital nurse, and his relationship to a young American patient named Chris. The two stories in actuality are separate chapters from Goyen's abandoned (or at least never published) novel, *Half a Look of Cain*. As stories they do not quite stand on their own as successfully as does "Figure Over the Town," also from that novel. Goyen recognizes they do not stand totally independently. Speaking of the novel from which they came, he wrote: "My work, whatever it is I do, is a shaping of patterns . . . and beyond that I do not know whether this work is and has been 'stories' or 'novels' or whatever. . . . I should like the whole to be like the patterns upon water because there has been a deep disturbance below." Of these two pieces, he pointed out they were not wholes in themselves, but rather hoped they "portended" the whole.[5] They are wonderfully strange and illuminating fictional pieces, indications that, in the writing of that particular novel, Goyen was diving more deeply into the subconscious than ever before.

Both are narrated by Curran, formerly a male nurse and now an old man with a crooked mind and a diminished body. Curran reminds one greatly of T. S. Eliot's Gerontion, particularly in the opening sections of "The Enchanted Nurse": "Now I speak at the end of a long time, and as someone old, for I am an old man sitting in a small room in a boardinghouse . . . it all comes to this, in the end, one voice in one small room telling what happened in many places and at many times in the broad world . . ." (p. 240).

"The Nurse" referred to in the one title is Curran himself, a servant to healing and to repair, and of the heart as well as of the body. "The Rescue" of the second title refers not so much to salvation from the flood which occurs in that tale as to human encounter. Goyen tells how "the meeting and coming together of two human beings is a rescue; and . . . lovelessness is a perishing" (p. 240). Both stories, as Richard Rhodes has remarked, work the margins that divide fiction from mythology. Both are curious, almost medieval, seeming to exist out of time and place, much like the gothic tales of Isak Dinesen. Rhodes cites in particular "The Rescue," with its hospital caught up in a flood that pulls in animals floating by from a flooded zoo.[6] This latter scene is surely one of Goyen's most fantastical, an entire peaceable kingdom occupying part of the hospital:

Still they came in as they were rescued out of the waters, all the peaceful animals, birds and even marvelous snakes who did not even show their wicked tongues, they were so grateful it seemed; and little blinking monkeys were brought in, sheep, every kind of animal you can imagine. And as they were led through the ward, they were mingled with the quiet and benign procession of the delicate wounded men, they all went out together. (p. 257)

The language, as can be seen, is almost trancelike. The hospital clearly is a microcosm of the macrocosm, a miniature world within the world, peopled not just by humans but by beasts as well. Chris's struggle for physical health and Curran's for emotional (with his mechanical apparatus he literally as well as figuratively works around the heart of Chris) are emblematic of man's condition. In an imperfect world, all seek a perfection rarely achieved but often sought in relationships with another. Such perfection is symbolized in the carnival act of "Gli Maravigliosi" (The Marvelous Ones), who perform an act of perfect grace and balance. The serenity they achieve amidst imperiled order parallels that of the tightrope walker Addis Adair, in Goyen's later *Come, the Restorer*. Like that wire act, something sensual as well as spiritual is achieved in the performance of The Marvelous Ones, liberating audience as well as performer.

Together these two tales are a surrealized and intellectualized study of the nature of love—love in its idealized form and the less ideal (one woman falls in love with a swan!). The human love triangle which begins in "The Enchanted Nurse" is never resolved in "The Rescue." The stories are incomplete. But they dazzle with their language and scenes of dream imagery. One is grateful Goyen chose to publish these audacious sections from the longer work.

V *"Tapioca Surprise"*

"Tapioca Surprise" is a confection, but a delicious one. It was first published in 1974, as Goyen's contribution to the *Bicentennial Collection of Texas Short Stories*. It is a comedy of supposed poisoning. Compared to the majority of the author's stories, it is weak in plot and characterization. Compared to "The Enchanted Nurse" and "The Rescue," it merely skates along the thin surface of its plot. And the point of view is highly misogynistic. Goyen here seems to be having fun at the expense of the whole female sex (as he perhaps did as well in "The White Rooster"). In this later story he tells us, "The ladies all sat around talking about their troubles and afflictions, the way they loved to do" (p. 272). One exchange of dialogue reads, " 'What is it?' somebody asked Lew Tully who was in, again, for a drying out. 'Beats me, but from what I can tell, somebody tried to poison and then rape twelve Paradisers.' 'Why'd he want to poison 'em?' 'Why'd he want to rape 'em?' answered Lew" (p. 276).

Nevertheless, the story zips along with a great deal of humor, reminiscent of the Goyen who wrote *The Fair Sister*, his most comedic novel. "Tapioca Surprise" has for its protagonist a Ms. Opal Ducharm, whose endless attempts to communicate over a phone which will not work recall Princis Lester (from "Zamour") and her own eternal wait for undelivered mail. Like Princis Lester, Opal Ducharm also possesses a cat of ambivalent affections. Unlike Princis Lester's tale, which one critic has perceived to be a comic version of Tennyson's "Lady of Shalott," Goyen's "Tapioca Surprise" yields no mythic implications. It exists "merely" to expose the foibles of certain southern ladies who live to socialize and socialize to live, ladies for whom gossip and hypochondria are ways of life. The story also pokes goodnatured fun at a region which would support an organization such as the Paradisers (who remind this writer of the Texas Rangerettes). It is Goyen's lightest tale, but also his funniest.

VI   *"Bridge of Music, River of Sand"*

"Bridge of Music, River of Sand" is at the time of this writing one of the most recent short stor.ies to be published by Goyen (it first appeared in the *Atlantic* in 1975), as well as one of his most elusive and poetic. A first-person narrative, it is a memory-piece and seems to be (like so much of Goyen) a lament for diminished things. The bridge of the title at one time spanned the grand and rolling Trinity River. Now only a trickle runs in its dry bed.

The story's central action is that of a naked diver's leap off the bridge and into the nonriver. His act is seen, but not comprehended by, the narrator. Had the figure committed suicide, or was his leap accidental? Could he have been pushed? How could he not know the riverbed was dry? As the narrator descends to the bed, he finds what surely must be one of Goyen's most disturbing images:

His hands must have cut through the wet sand, carving a path for his head and shoulders. He was up to his mid-waist and had fallen to a kneeling position: a figure on its knees with its head buried in the sand, as if it had decided not to look at the world anymore. And then the figure began to sink as if someone underground were pulling it under. Slowly the stomach, lean and hairy, vanished; then the loins, thighs. The river, which had swallowed half this body, now seemed to be eating the rest of it. For a while the feet lay, soles up, on the sand. And then they went down, arched like a dancer's. (pp. 281–82)

A strange figure. The narrator wonders whether it could be that of some tormented spirit—another of Goyen's ghosts—doomed forever to reenact his suicide, continuing it now, even with the river dried and gone. Whatever, it disappeared totally, taken in by the mud.

Goyen concludes the story with a kind of coda, in which the narrator drives on toward his old home, his eyes smarting from the fumes of a mill which pollutes the air. Within these few pages, then, we perceive the ruination of at least two of our natural elements and resources, the waterways and the air. The diving figure is like Icarus, only in reverse: seeking escape from the dangers of this world, he plunges downward rather than upward; into mud rather than air.

The bridge from which he leaps symbolizes, perhaps, that link between what can be perceived and what is beyond perception.

(Recall that the Roman Pontiff, as the etymology of his name suggests, is a kind of bridge between God and Man.) Even if Goyen did not intend this mystic sense of the story, in most cultures the bridge has been symbolic of a transition from one state to another—of change or of the desire for a change. Goyen's visiting narrator is changing from his new environment back to his old, while the landscape has changed from the old to the new:

It was a heat-stunned afternoon. The July heat throbbed. The blue, steaming air waved like a veil. The feeling of something missing haunted me: it was the lost life of the river—something so powerful that it had haunted the countryside for miles around; you could feel it a long time before you came to it. In a landscape that was unnatural—flowing water was missing—everything else seemed unnatural. (p. 281)

The dried-up river symbolizes loss of fertility and lack of progressiveness in the land. The disappearing leaper ultimately is symbolic of loss and of oblivion. As Louis K. MacKendrick wrote, the story "confronts the mystery and decay of beauty in a memorable single image, exact and cryptic."[8]

Goyen himself has attempted to explain the story, concluding, "I haven't a clue as to what the story means. It is surely about loss (in spirit). Yet despite loss, mystery and beauty remain. . . . This seems to be a sudden vision of my life, out of memory (it's a real place—in Riverside, Texas, just outside Trinity; the bridge was real, the trestle was real, those were my parents and sister, the incident was real). It was out of this sudden vision that the story was written in one writing."[9]

VII *"Figure Over the Town"*

"Figure Over the Town" is an equally disturbing story, and a more fully developed one. Originally written as part of *Half a Look of Cain*, it stands superbly on its own as a superior, distinct tale. It has already been anthologized numerous times since its first appearance in the *Saturday Evening Post* (1963).

The story begins in the middle of its action: "In the town of my beginning I saw this masked figure sitting aloft. It was never explained to me by my elders, who were thrilled and disturbed by the figure, too, who it was, except that he was called Flagpole

Moody" p. 285). As developed by the author, Flagpole Moody was the conflict of an idea with a society; an idea bred by the society—raised up there, even, by the society—"in short, society was in the flagpole sitter and he was in the society of the town" (p. 293.)

Like "Bridge of Music, River of Sand," this, too, is a memory story, yet one experienced by a child, and including comments and thoughts that could pass only through the mind of an adult.[10] The point of view is that of childhood as filtered through the memory and the experience of an adult. This duality is required to give dimension to the story—to first give the events as perceived by the child, and then to interpret them through worldly, adult knowledge.

The story's development is largely a tracing of the town's attitude toward Flagpole Moody from the townspeople's first attempts to discover his reason for sitting on the pole to the time they mock him by staging a wartime carnival at the very base of his pole and setting up a Ferris wheel to circle beneath his very nose. Each change is wrought through incomprehension of his position. The boy's mother at first thinks the sitter's stunt is foolish; later she decides it is morbid; at one point the town ignores him; at another they become disturbed by him. For some he is a figure of desire, like the other-worldly Mr. de Persia, of *Come, the Restorer*; for others he is a tramp and an anti-Christ. Obviously, he is intended to serve as all things to all men. As Goyen writes,

Everybody used Flagpole Moody for his own purpose, and so he, sitting away from it all, apparently serene in his own dream and idea of himself, became the lost lover to the lovelorn, the saint to the seekers of salvation, the scapegoat of the guilty, the damned to those who were lost. (p. 290)

The key phrase here is *serene in his own dream and idea of himself*. Flagpole Moody is like Jim Coopers of "The Thief Coyote" and like Mr. Stevens of "Tenant in the Garden." And what this town cannot tolerate is that Moody *is* moody, that he has a vision, a purpose which they do not comprehend and cannot tolerate because it is different from theirs. Read on this level, "Figure Over the Town" is an allegorical story of the artist as flagpole sitter—in society, yet above it all, misunderstood and spurned by it. Like Noah in the biblical story to which the narrator alludes, Moody is a survivor of the storm. The artists and inventors in our midst are all "flagpole sitters" and often just as unjustifiably debased.

Flagpole Moody's withdrawal from society is apparently a success. He comes down only in his own time, when he wants to come down; he withstands all earlier requests and jeers. Further, his act has changed someone, as all good works of art are capable of doing. His act, his differentness, have captured the imagination of the boy-narrator. He has caused the boy to aspire toward loftier things, toward a heroism or an individuality of his own. It is no accident that Goyen places his hero above the others. And in his own magnificent dream of Flagpole Moody, the boy enters the man's abandoned pole tent to make the place his own. He even attempts to piece together, with infinite care, the fragments of letters there, to see what they told, to comprehend Moody's existence, to make whole cloth out of the chaos which is this world. It is a highly symbolic action for the novitiate artist. Like all works of art, this one too begins in a dream and ends in the world.

Like Shirley Jackson's classic story "The Lottery," Goyen's allegorical tale is a revelation of certain characteristics of society. Restless, impatient, intolerent, often destructive, society will not let the creative peacefully coexist with the uncreative. Yet Goyen, the adult narrator as author, continues in his life and work to be a flagpole sitter in America today.

CHAPTER 10

A Literature of Sensibility

"IT is easier in our society to be naked physically than to be naked psychologically or spiritually," Rollo May writes in his seminal little book, *The Courage to Create*.[1] And May is correct in his evaluation of our contemporary society, in which people find it easier to share their bodies than their fantasies. For whatever reason, until fairly recently, fiction writers found the sharing of their hopes, fears, and aspirations as marking them as too vulnerable. They were shy about sharing those things which matter most. Novels by Joyce and Lawrence and Miller were exceptions, of course: but the most daring of their productions were outlawed. It was only, perhaps, with the advent of such liberated novels as Philip Roth's *Portnoy's Complaint* (1969) and Erica Jong's *Fear of Flying* (1973) that the courage to create publicly became as unbridled as the courage to copulate.

But not so with William Goyen. From the first—that is, roughly from 1949 onward—his fiction has been of the most intimate kind, surpassing the physical realities in favor of the subjective ones. Events, when they occur in his fiction at all, are related not to character so much as to sensibility. His concern is not for concrete truths, but poetic truths—for the dream, the fantasy, the outrageous. It is this engagement with *all* things, not merely the physical things of this world, which is a part of Goyen's real achievement. It is what gives his work its vast range. It is why a novel about a small town in Texas can appeal to thousands of readers, not just in this country, but also in France, Germany, England, Italy, and Spain. It is why his tales, full of East Texas vernacular, rise above mere regionalism.

As one of Goyen's best critics, Patrice Repusseau, has written, Goyen's works "are but a foil for an inner journey into self, an erotic and mystic probing of memory, with universal meaning."[2] Repusseau rightly calls *The House of Breath* "a ceaseless dialogue between now and then, between what is and what used to be, between wanderings and home." The book is also a reflection on the human condition ("how each man holds within himself the burden of ancestry, and how he cannot get rid of the obsessing faces of blood kindred") and on the failure of human communication. ("There is always a chasm between human beings, even lovers, and the bridges spanning the islands of solitude are as fragile as a web of breath.")

Another astute critic of Goyen's writings, Robert K. Morris, declares, "William Goyen has seized upon those tangible manifestations of life to present his own transcendental vision of the fragile, yet enduring, human condition."[3]

In the past several chapters of this little book, I have made allusion to films by Fellini. In an interview, appearing in the *New York Times* in 1965, Fellini stated his artistic purposes. They could, I contend, stand for Goyen's as well. Fellini said,

. . . I want to bring in pieces of the different dreams I have had during my life. The faces, the gardens, the squares, the towns, all the places I have visited during the night. To show how people are deeply alone. It is very exciting. There is something very decadent and something very innocent at the same time. Strength and weakness. Like a baby covered with dust.

In attempting to cover a panorama of his day- and night-mares, Goyen has created a large gallery of characters. Unlike many very subjective novelists who can write only about themselves (Jean Rhys, Denton Welch), Goyen has created, or recreated, young girls and old men; the ordinary and the freakish; the famous and the obscure; the military and the civilian; the country and the urban; the straight and the gay. His characters even include animals and trees, and a good many ghosts as well as flesh.

In addition to his sharp and varied characterizations, there is, of course, his fine ear. The vernacular employed in his stories is flawless, as any Southwesterner could tell you. This concern for speech is but a part of his whole concern for language—precise, detailed, telling. A passage from a Goyen book is, ultimately, so individual it could have been written by no one else.

Then there are Goyen's topics, which, if dealing primarily with exile and suppression of individuals and individuality, also take a large overview and nearly always, in some way, deal with ecology, with the diminished and the lost things of this world.

The body of William Goyen's work does not vary greatly in quality. *A Book of Jesus* is an oddity and slight. In the realm of his fiction, if one had to "do without" one book, I suppose the comedic *The Fair Sister* is disposable—though one would doubtless miss Savata, Ruby, and Canaan. That these are late books does not mean Goyen's creative powers failed after the first. Indeed, the number of references to *Come, the Restorer* in this study alone should indicate some measure of that novel's originality and importance. The recent stories at the back of his *Collected Stories* are further displays of strength and vision. Overall, his work is consistent and at a very high level. And *The House of Breath* is perhaps a masterpiece—still in print twenty-five years after publication.

Nevertheless, it is doubtful that Goyen's fiction has been a creditable influence upon any other writer of note today. His concerns and his style are too highly individual to be of use by others. (Anyone who has attempted to copy his style will find that task near impossible). Rather than being famous as the founder of a school or a following, Goyen should be noted as a highly individualized voice. He is a fabulous original, like Carson McCullers and Flannery O'Connor and not many others. In an age of mechanization, he devotes himself to poetry. In an age of plastic, he celebrates the ghost and the flesh.

Interview with William Goyen
by Robert Phillips

*The interview with William Goyen took place on a sunny Saturday after-
noon in June 1975—the spring of Goyen's sixtieth birthday and also of the
publication of the twenty-fifth-anniversary-edition of his first novel,* The
House of Breath.

*Taped over a three-hour period in the home of a friend in Katonah, New
York, Mr. Goyen remained seated on a sofa throughout the interview, sip-
ping a soft drink. He requested that baroque music be played over the
stereo, "to break the silences." There were silences—long, considering
pauses between thoughts.*

*William Goyen is slender, lanky, and a handsome figure at sixty. His
aspect is intense and patrician, his manner gracious and courtly. Goyen's
hair is silver: he speaks with a strong Southwestern accent.*

INTERVIEWER: In the Introduction to your *Selected Writings*, you stated
that you began writing at the age of sixteen, at a time when you were also
interested in composing and dancing and other art forms. Why writing as a
career rather than one of the other arts?

GOYEN: My foremost ambition, as a very young person, was to be a
composer, but my father was strongly opposed to my studying music—that
was for girls. He was from a sawmill family who made strict a division
between a male's work and a female's. (The result was quite a confusion of
sex-roles in later life: incapable men and oversexed women among his own
brothers and sisters.) He was so violently against my studying music that he
would not allow me even to play the piano in our house. Only my sister was
allowed to put a finger to the keyboard . . . the piano had been bought for
her. My sister quickly tired of her instrument, and when my father was
away from the house, I merrily played away, improving upon my sister's
Etudes—which I had learned by ear—and indulging in grand Mozartian
fantasies. In the novel *The House of Breath*, Boy Ganchion secretly plays a
"cardboard piano," a paper keyboard pasted on a piece of cardboard in a
hidden corner. I actually did this as a boy. My mother secretly cut it out of

115

the local newspaper and sent off a coupon for beginners' music lessons. I straightaway devised Lisztlike concerti and romantic overtures. And so silent arts were mine: I began writing. No one could hear that, or know that I was doing it, even as with the cardboard piano.

INTERVIEWER: You weren't having to write under the sheets with a flashlight, were you?

GOYEN: You know, I *was* playing my music under the quilt at night, quite literally. I had a little record player and I played what music I could under the quilt and later wrote that way. So I did write under the sheets.

INTERVIEWER: What was your father's reaction to writing?

GOYEN: Something of the same. He discovered it some years later, when I was an undergraduate at Rice University in Houston. He found me writing plays, and to him the theater, like the piano, was an engine of corruption which bred effeminate men (God knows he was generally right, I came to see), sexual libertines (right again!), and a band of gypsies flaunting their shadowed eyes and tinseled tights at reality. When my first novel was published, my father's fears and accusations were justified—despite the success of the book—and he was outraged to the point of not speaking to me for nearly a year.

This could, of course, have been because the book was mostly about his own family—the sawmill family I spoke of earlier. My father, his brothers, his father, everybody else were lumber people, around mills . . . and forests. I went around the sawmills with him, you see, and saw all that. He loved trees so! My God, he would . . . he'd just *touch* trees . . . they were human beings. He would smell wood and trees. He just loved them. He knew wood. He was really meant for that.

Poor beloved man, though, he later came around to my side and became the scourge of local bookstores, making weekly rounds to check their stock of my book. He must have bought a hundred copies for his lumbermen friends. God knows what *they* thought of it. Before he died he had become my ardent admirer, and my *Selected Writings* is dedicated to him.

INTERVIEWER: Do you agree with the theory that an unhappy childhood is essential to the formation of exceptional gifts? Were you genuinely unhappy?

GOYEN: How could it have been any other way? My own nature was one that would have made it that way. It was a melancholy childhood. It was a childhood that was searching for—or that *needed*—every kind of compensation it could get. I think that's what makes an artist. So that I looked for compensation to fulfill what was not there.

INTERVIEWER: How have the physical conditions of your writing changed over the years? What is the relation between the creative act and privacy for you, today? In your *Note* on the twenty-fifth-anniversary-edition of *The House of Breath*, you stated that part of the novel was written on an aircraft carrier in the Pacific.

GOYEN: Since my writing began in the air of secrecy, indeed, of aliena-tion—as the work had to be done without anyone's knowing it—forever after my work has had about it the air of someone in solitude having done it, alienated from the press of society and the everyday movements of life.

On the ship, where I continued working, I found that there are many hidden places on an aircraft carrier where one can hide out and do secret work. And this was easily achieved. Also on the night watches and so forth, there was a lot of time. There is a great deal of free time aboard a ship in wartime, ironically. This kind of tradition in my work has been mine all my life, and I have generally lived in hidden places. In New Mexico it was at the beautiful foot of a mountain (the Sangre de Cristo in the primitive village of El Prado), and also in a mysterious mountain (Kiowa Mountain— the D. H. Lawrence Ranch called Kiowa Ranch, over San Cristobal, New Mexico, near Taos). And in Europe—Zurich, Rome—I worked in backstreet *pensions*.

Yet more and more, as I get more worldly and have the security of having survived, I feel that it is not necessary to be *that* far removed from the workings of daily life and the daily lives of people. Indeed, the older I get and the more I write, the more I feel it important to be a part of daily life . . . to know that it surrounds me as I work. I presently live in a large apartment on the West Side of New York City. One of those rooms is mine, and it's an absolute hideaway, yet all around me in the other rooms the life of a family goes on, and I like to know that. I also like to know that twelve flights down I can step onto the street in the midst of a lot of human beings and feel a part of those. Whereas, in the old days, in New Mexico, I was brought up—taught by—Frieda Lawrence to see that simple manual en-deavor is part of art. I would work in gardens and dig water ditches and walk in mountains and along rivers when I was not writing, and I felt that it was absolutely essential to my work. That's changing for me now. I'm more city-prone. Maybe the world is changing, too. Maybe solitude is best had in the midst of multitudes.

It's amazing how quickly something gets written. Now, when it comes, it can be on a bus, or in a store. I've stopped in Macy's and written on a dry-goods counter and then suddenly had a whole piece of writing for myself that was accomplished, where earlier in my life I felt I had to spend a week in a house somewhere in order to get that. Conditions change.

INTERVIEWER: Some say that poverty is ennobling to the soul. Is economic stability helpful to a writer? On the other hand, do you think wealth can be harmful?

GOYEN: It can be harmful. This depends on the stage in a writer's life, of course. As a young man, for me . . . I speak now not as a wealthy or an impoverished man, but as a man looking back when he was younger . . . it was imperative that I live *very* simply and economically. Living in Taos where—who would have believed it then fifteen or twenty years later, a whole migration of young hippies would come to live and meditate in the desert just where I had lived—I was totally solitary. It was imperative for me and my work that I keep everything simple and have practically nothing at all. I lived in just a mud house with a dirt floor on land that Frieda Lawrence gave me out of friendship. I built it with a friend and a couple of Indians. Yet, to live in absolute poverty all his life could harm a writer's work. The hardship and worry over money in writers as they get older is a social horror; grants given to writers should be *sufficient*, so that they are able to live with amplitude and, yes, some dignity.

INTERVIEWER: The genesis of it all goes back to that aircraft carrier, doesn't it?

GOYEN: I thought I was going to die in the war. I was on a terrible ship. It was the *Casablanca*, the first baby flattop. There were always holes in it, and people dying and it was just the worst place for me to be. I really was desperate. I just wanted to jump off. I thought I was going to die anyway, be killed, and I wanted to die because I couldn't endure what looked like an endless way of life with which I had nothing to do—the war, the ship, and the water . . . I have been terrified of water all my life. I would have fits when I got close to it.
     Suddenly—it was out on a deck in the cold—I saw the breath that came from me. And I thought that the simplest thing that I know is what I belong to and where I came from and I just called out to my family as I stood there that night, and it just . . . I saw this breath come from me and I thought—in that breath, in that call, is *their* existence, is their reality . . . and I must shape that and I must write about them—*The House of Breath*.
     I saw this whole thing. I saw what was going to be four, five years' work. Isn't that amazing? But I knew it was there. Many of my stories happen that way. It's dangerous to tell my students this because then these young people say, "Gee, all I've got to do, if I really want to write, is wait around for some ship in the cold night, and I'll blow out my breath, and I've got my thing."

INTERVIEWER: So this sustained you?

GOYEN: It brought my life back to me. I saw my relationships; it was extraordinary. Lost times come for us in our lives if we're not phony and if we just listen; it hurts, but it's also very joyous and beautiful . . . it's a redemption . . . it's all those things that we try to find and the world seems to be looking for . . . as a matter of fact, that's the *hunger* of the world. So there it was on the ship and it just came to me. I saw so much . . . that I wouldn't have to go home and they wouldn't have to suffocate me; they wouldn't kill me; I'd find other relationships.

INTERVIEWER: So after the war you didn't go home.

GOYEN: When the war was over, I just dipped into Texas and got my stuff and left and headed towards San Francisco. I had come to love San Francisco when it was the home port for my ship, the aircraft carrier, and I thought that it would be a good place to live. But I passed through Taos, New Mexico, in winter, in February, and I was enchanted. It really was like an Arthurian situation . . . I couldn't leave. It was beautiful and remote, like a Himalayan village, untouched, with this adobe color that was ruby-colored and yellow, all the magical colors of mud. It's not all one color. It's like Rome. Rome looks like that. And the sunlight and the snow . . . just about everyone on foot . . . a few cars . . . high, 7,500 feet.

INTERVIEWER: Did the D. H. Lawrence commune in Taos have anything to do with your staying?

GOYEN: I didn't know anything about the Lawrence legend. Had I, I might not have stayed at all. But I did, and right away I thought that I'd better get a little more money for myself before I settled in to work. So I got a job as a waiter at a very fashionable inn called Sagebrush Inn. I worked as a waiter for a few months until I met Frieda, who came in one night and I waited on her. The whole Lawrence world came to dinner there: Dorothy Brett and Mabel Dodge, Spud Johnson, Tennessee Williams: he was living up at the ranch. They all came to my table. And then the owner of the Inn had to come out and say, this young man is just out of the war and he wants to be a writer. The *worst* thing I wanted said about me; it almost paralyzed me. Well, of course, Tennessee thought, oh, God, who cares about *another* writer. But Frieda, said, you must come and have tea with me. She said it right away. I went and from that moment . . . we just hit it off. It was almost a love affair. It was the whole world.

So it wasn't Lawrence that brought me to her; circumstances brought me to Frieda and I found her a great pal and a luminous figure in my life on her own terms.

I would go to teas with her. She would have high teas. In Texas we had a Coke. But here it was the first time I met someone who baked bread, you know? She made a cake and brought it out . . . it was wonderful. She wore German clothes, like dirndles, and peasant outfits, and an apron. She was a kitchen frau. A few people came . . . Mabel Dodge had given her this great 300-acre ranch in return for the manuscript of *Sons and Lovers*. That was the exchange. Except she never took *Sons and Lovers* away, so that the manuscript and many others, *Women in Love*, all holograph . . . were there in a little cupboard at the ranch. I could read them and look at them in amazement.

INTERVIEWER: What sort of things did you talk about?

GOYEN: We talked about the simplest things . . . well, really about love, about men and women and about sex, about *physical* living. Of course, I didn't know that I was hearing what Lawrence had heard. Because it was Frieda who gave Lawrence this whole thing and it overwhelmed me.

The various people would come up in the summer and spend time with us, all kinds of people. Just simple people; Indians . . . she was close to Indians. I got very close to three Indians who were really like my family and helped me build my house.

INTERVIEWER: And then people like Tennessee Williams came.

GOYEN: Yes, Tennessee stayed up there with his friend, Frank Merlo. Tennessee told us that he heard Lawrence's voice . . . he was a haunted poor thing, but he did go a little too far. D. H. Lawrence was whispering things to him. Suddenly Tennessee had a terrible stomach ache and it turned out that he had a very bad appendix and had to be brought down to Mabel Dodge. Mabel owned the only hospital; built it and owned it. It was like a European town and we were the only Americans, and I went to this hospital to witness Tennessee's dying . . . he was always dying, you know. He was dying in this Catholic hospital screaming four-letter words and all kinds of things with the nuns running around wearing the most enormous habits, most unsanitary for a hospital. Mabel was wringing her hands and saying, "He's a genius, he's a genius." The doctor said, "I don't care; he's going to die, he's got gangrene. His appendix has burst. We have to operate at once." Tennessee said, "Not until I make my will." The doctor said, "How long will the will be?" "Well, everything's going to Frankie," so they sat down, with Frank going through an inventory of all Tennessee's possessions. "What about the house in Rome? You left that out." Tennessee was just writhing in pain. So they made a list of all the things. And then they wheeled him off and he indeed had this operation which to everyone's surprise he managed to recover from. Eventually he got out of there. . . .

INTERVIEWER: All this time you were working on *The House of Breath*. How did it get published?

GOYEN: It got published through Stephen Spender, indirectly. He came to that little village where I was living. I had sent a piece of it to *Accent*, a wonderful early magazine; it caused quite a kind of thing. I began to get letters. Random House wrote me a letter and said that they hoped this was "part of a book." (All editors do that, I later learned.) They'll say that even if it's just a "letter to the editor" they've seen. That's what editors have to do, God bless them, and I'm glad they do. About that time, Spender, a man I scarcely knew, whose *poetry* I scarcely knew, arrived in Taos on a reading tour. A wealthy lady named Helene Wurlitzer of the family who made the organs lived there and brought people into that strange territory to read, and give chamber concerts and so on. I never went to those things because . . . well, I didn't have any shoes; I really was living on mud floors in an adobe house that I had built, utterly primitive, which I loved. I was isolated and terrified with all those things going on in me . . . but I was writing that book. Well, Spender heard that I was there . . . he heard through Frieda, who went to the reading, and so then he asked me if he could come to see me; he treated me as though I were an important writer. He had just read that piece in *Accent* and he asked if there was more that he could read. I showed him some other pieces and he sent those around. They were published and then somebody at Random House sent me a contract right away of $250 advance for the book, and then promptly was fired. But Spender was very moved by the way I was living there; he wrote a well-known essay called "The Isolation of the American Writer" about my situation there. Nothing would do until Mr. Spender would have me come to London because he thought I was too isolated, too Texan, too hicky. . . . He really took it upon himself to make that kind of decision for me. It was a wonderful thing that he did. The stipulation was that I would bring a girl who had come into my life with me (this blessed girl had passed on among the leaves of autumn) and she was very much a part of my life there in London and together we were real vagabonds, embarrassing everybody—people like Stephen, and Cyril Connolly, and Elizabeth Bowen, Rose Macaulay, I mean, all of them. . . .

INTERVIEWER; You stayed in Spender's house?

GOYEN: I had a room at the top and Dorothy had a room in the basement, with the stairs between us, creaking stairs. It was an elegant house, an eighteenth-century house in St. John's Wood. At 4:00 tea time in the winter it was dark, and they pulled Florentine-brocaded curtains and turned on lights; it was a time of austerity still, but people came to tea. Veronica Wedgewood would arrive. Dorothy wouldn't come up from the basement. She really hated this kind of thing. She vanished. She just wouldn't participate. So I was really quite alone with this. I guess I must have kept her under wraps. I must have been very bad to her. I don't know. I have to think about that some time. But here they would come: Natasha, Stephen's wife, who was a gifted pianist and wanted to be a concert pianist, and so musicians came, and painters. Cyril Connolly was often there because he and Stephen were working together. Dame Edith Sitwell came. We went to

122 of 164 WILLIAM GOYEN

her house and she read one night; she sat behind a screen because she wouldn't read facing anyone or a group . . . behind a marvelous Chinese screen and you would hear this voice coming through the screen . . . all those people . . . that was a world that Spender gave me and was a great influence in my life and on my work.

INTERVIEWER: What an extraordinary change.

GOYEN: I was thrown into this elegant environment which was precisely the opposite of what I had been doing. It was right for me because my character, Folner, yearned for elegance. Suddenly my country people were singing out their despair in those great elegant houses. I saw cathedrals for the first time . . . I'd not really seen cathedrals . . . I was able to get to Paris and all around there. All this went into *The House of Breath*. I saw the Sistine Chapel—well, that's the first page of *The House of Breath*, "on the dome of my skull, paradises and infernos and annunciations" and so forth. Europe just put it all right—everything that started in a little town in Texas, you see. It saved the book, I think. Because it made that cry, you know . . . it is an *elegant cry* . . . there's nothing better than an elegant cry of despair. . . .

INTERVIEWER: Did people worry what this tremendous change in *venue*—from Taos to Europe—would do to *The House of Breath?*

GOYEN: Some people worried about it. James Laughlin of *New Directions*, when I had published a bit, wrote me, "You are ruining your work fast; the influences you are coming into are coming too soon, and you're allowing your personality to overwhelm your talent. Obviously people find your *Texas* personality . . ." (and he could be a snide guy, too) ". . . charming and you might be of interest to them for a little while. But you are writing a very serious book and this will be permanently damaging to your work." He really wanted me to get out of there.

INTERVIEWER: Were there other Cassandras about *The House of Breath?*

GOYEN: Well, Auden had kind of looked down his nose at me. He said it's the kind of writing where the next page is more beautiful than the one just read. "One is just breathless for fear that you're not going to be able to do it," he said, "and that makes me too nervous. I prefer James."

   Christopher Isherwood said, "You know, my dear boy, you'll never make it. That is what one feels when one reads you. You'll never survive with this kind of sensibility unless you change, get some armor on yourself." As a matter of fact, he wrote me and warned me again . . . he put it all down in a letter. And that *did* scare me. I was young and I was scared. But I knew that I had no choice. Then that feeling of doom *really* came on me . . . because I had no choice. I knew that I couldn't write any other way.

INTERVIEWER: When you began writing *The House of Breath* did you expect it to be published? Were you writing for publication?

GOYEN: I was most surely not "writing for publication." But I don't think there is any piece of the novel except one that was not published in magazines before the book itself was published.

INTERVIEWER: You said earlier your father was upset by the book when it was published. Had you been concerned about the family and hometown reaction?

GOYEN: Concerned, yes. I fell out of favor with many people in the town, let's put it that way, and just about disinherited by my own family. I had nasty letters, bad letters from home, and heart-broken letters from my mother and my father. Generally the attitude was one of hurt and shock. It was not until fifteen years later that I was able to go back to the town! And even then rather snide remarks were made to me by the funeral director and by the head of the bank. We met on the street.

INTERVIEWER: So when you apply for a loan, you won't do it in that town?

GOYEN: No, and I won't die there, either.

INTERVIEWER: How long did you and the girl stay as Spender's guests in England?

GOYEN: I settled in for the whole year of 1949 . . . and I finished the book in that house at St. John's Wood, in Stephen's house. The girl was there until it got very bad; we had problems and so she moved to Paris; that made me have to go to Paris to see her there and we had this kind of thing that was going on. When I came back, bringing my manuscript on the *Queen Mary*, she came with me to New York. But then we had one visit with Bob Linscott, my editor, who said to her, "My dear, do you like to eat? Do you like a roof over your head? You'll never have it; he's an artist. I feed him and Random House has kept him alive and probably will have to from now on. Don't marry him, don't even fall in love" . . . and he broke her heart. He really did. Poor Dorothy. He was right; I wasn't about to be saddled down. And so it broke away and that's OK. Many years later I found a woman exactly like her. Her name was Doris, and so often I say to Doris, "Dorothy," and I'm in trouble.

INTERVIEWER: That was quite a step for an editor to take. What do you think their particular function should be?

GOYEN: Well, really caring for authors . . . not meddling with what they did but loving them so much and letting them know that he cares. Generally at that point, when you're starting, you feel that nobody does. Linscott looked after you and if you had no money, he gave you money. Once Truman Capote met me at the Oak Room of the Plaza. "I'm embarrassed to sit with you," he said when I sat down, "your suit is terrible." I hadn't really thought about what I was wearing. He said, "I'm not going to have you wear that suit anymore. But," he said, "I've ordered drinks for us and if you'll just wait, I'm going to call Bob and tell him that he must buy you a suit that costs at least $250." And he did. Bob gave me money and he told me, "Well, I guess he's right." He was lovable, Truman. He did sweet lovely things then.

INTERVIEWER: Carson McCullers was one of Linscott's authors, wasn't she?

GOYEN: I had first known her in this nest that Linscott had up there for these little birdlings of writers. Carson had great vitality and she was quite beautiful in that already decaying way. She was like a fairy. She had the most delicate kind of tinkling, dazzling little way about her . . . like a little star. Like a Christmas, she was like an ornament of a kind. She had no mind and she could make no philosophical statements about anything; she didn't need to. She said far-out, wonderfully mad things, that were totally disarming and for a while people would say, "I'll go wherever you go." She'd knock them straight out the window.

INTERVIEWER: What sort of people interested her?

GOYEN: She had a devastating crush on Elizabeth Bowen. She actually got to Bowen's Court: she shambled over there to England and spent a fortnight. I heard from Elizabeth that Carson appeared at dinner the first night in her shorts, tennis shorts; that poor body, you know, in tennis shorts and she came down the stairs; that was her debut. It didn't last long. But that was Carson.

INTERVIEWER: What was distinctive about her stories—as, say, compared to the other Southern "magnolia" writers?

GOYEN: She would try to make her stories scary, and the word "haunted" was used, of course, by the literary critics, "the haunted domain." I think that was the French title for Truman's first novel . . . *Other Voices, Other Rooms. Les Domaines Hantés.* But Carson was . . . she was a really truly lost, haunted wonder-creature. It's hard to be that and grow old, because of course you either go mad out of what you see, or I guess you try to imitate that kind of purity. She was a bad imitator. So it was just a bore.

INTERVIEWER: She was not a person to have as an enemy.

GOYEN: She was . . . not tough but she had a nasty . . . well, she had a way of absolutely devastating you; the kind that hurt, that little kind of peeping "drop dead" sort of thing. She had an eye for human frailty and would go right to that; that's why people fled her. They thought, who needs this? Why be around her?

Then, of course, she was terribly affected by not being able to write. It was a murderous thing, a death blow, that block. She said she just didn't have anything to write. And really, it was as though she had never written. This happens to writers when there are dead spells. We die sometimes. And it's as though we're in a tomb; it's death. That's what we all fear, and that's why so many of us become alcoholics or suicides or insane—or just no-good philanderers. It's amazing that we survive, though I think survival in some cases is kind of misgiven and it's a bore. It was written recently about Saul Bellow that one of the best things about him is that he survived, he didn't become an alcoholic, he didn't go mad, and so forth. And that the true heroism of him lies simply in his endurance. That's the way we look at artists in America. People said to me when I was sixty, "My God, you're one of the ones, how are you? But you look *wonderful*. We didn't know where you were." They thought I was dead, or in an institution or something.

INTERVIEWER: Could her editor Linscott help McCullers at all?

GOYEN: Poor Linscott couldn't get any more out of her and then he died before he could help her. I doubt whether he could have; no one could have. She was hopeless. She was just kind of a little expendable thing, you know? She would stay with me days at a time. I put her to bed; she had a little nightgown. I was playing sort of dolly; I was playing house. I sat with her while her ExLax worked. Two or three chocolate ExLaxes and three wine glasses, and about three Seconal. And I would sit by her bed and see that it all worked, or at least it all got going in her. And then she was off to sleep.

She had some awful cancer of the nerve ends. This caused the strokes, and she had a stroke finally on the other side until she was very badly paralyzed and then she had just a massive, killing stroke. She was absolute skin and bones. They took her down there to Georgia, not far from where Flannery O'Connor lived, where they buried her.

INTERVIEWER: Could she have written an autobiography?

GOYEN: She did not have "a hold of herself," as a person would say, enough to look back and see herself in situations. She never could have written her autobiography; it would be impossible for her . . . she had disguised herself so much . . . And what a past, you know? Her mother . . . the Mother of *all* these people . . . thank God mine seems to be quite okay—I'd be raving mad at this point. Carson's mother was an aggressive lady, all over the place, and she came here once and worked at *Mademoiselle*. She had a notorious time as a fiction editor there. She did the oddest things . . . rejecting stories in her own Georgian way, generally in terms of cooking. I think she wrote to a writer once, "The crust of this story holds its contents well . . . " (she was off on a pie), "but my dear, by the time we get to the custard, it runs." The pie image went on and on. "This pie won't do," she said, " . . . came out of the oven too soon." She was a self-educated lady from the South who very early on had read Katherine Mansfield, for instance, and had told Carson about Mansfield, which was the worst thing she could have done. Once I went with her to meet Carson's plane. When she saw her daughter step out of the plane, she turned to me and said, "I seen the little lamp." I thought, "That's some allusion I'm going to have to find out about." When Carson reached us, she said, "Carson, you know what I told Bill when you appeared?" (She was the kind of lady who would repeat a thing she'd said.) "I told him that I seen the little lamp." Carson burst into tears. I said, "Please tell me what this is that hurts you so." She said, "Well, it's that beautiful story called 'The Doll's House' by Katherine Mansfield. It's the last line of the story. A poor little girl peeks in a garden at a doll's house owned by a snobbish family, and she sees this glowing little lamp inside. Later when the little girl's sister asks why there is a curious glow in her eye, she says, 'I seen the little lamp.' "

INTERVIEWER: What about your own mother?

GOYEN: As a literary person I truly am the offspring of my mother and women like my mother. There's no woman like a Texas woman in her eighties. It's not southern. She wouldn't have a clue as to what a "southern lady" was. Hers was a singing way of expressing things, and this I heard so very early that it became my own speech; that's the way I write. I love spending money to talk to her on the phone in Texas an hour at a time because it's just as though the curtain that came down on an opera last night goes right up when I call her tonight. The aria goes right on; it's just wonderful.

INTERVIEWER: What do you talk about?

GOYEN: About how Houston has grown, and how she wants to go back to the little town she left fifty years ago. I write her expressions down; I have to do that to understand what they really mean; it's almost another language. But she keeps breeding it. I mean, she's writing all the time. I may not be writing, but she is. She's alive . . . .

INTERVIEWER: Do you carry a notebook with you to put these things in? Or keep a diary?

GOYEN: Oh yes, I always carry paper with me . . . something to write on, always. And I keep not so much a formal diary any longer, but, well, it's a notebook, and in it I keep most things.

INTERVIEWER: What do you do with those ideas that strike you in the middle of Macy's, say, and you can't record them fully or easily? Are they often unrelated to what you currently are writing?

GOYEN: It's rarely unrelated. When one's really engaged deeply in a piece of work, truly writing it, it takes over almost everything else and you find you're thinking about it constantly and it's a part of everything that happens. Even the clerk in Macy's suddenly speaks out of the novel that you are writing, it seems, or is a character in it. All the people in the world are suddenly characters in the novel you are writing. Everything contributes. The created piece of work has suddenly replaced what is called real life . . . life as it really is, whatever *that* means . . . so that it's not surprising to have it come at one from all angles.

Therefore, I know that if I've been writing all morning and I've got to buy groceries at noon, I better take paper with me, because I'm going to *keep* writing as I go down the street; you can write on the sack that your groceries come in, and I have!

INTERVIEWER: What about the six years you were an editor at McGraw-Hill? Were you able to write, or did this interfere with your work?

GOYEN: The whole McGraw-Hill period is one that I want to write about. I have been writing about it in my *Memoirs* (my next book). The writer in the world of publishing, and particularly *me* in the world of publishing, who had been so disillusioned and embittered by publishers . . .

INTERVIEWER: You were disillusioned with your own publishers?

GOYEN: Not my own *per se*. Just publishing in general—the making of books and the life of the making of books. All these things seemed so dead-end to me, without meaning. In this great place, this huge publishing house, I was a special person, in that I was a special editor. I was brought there to concern myself with serious writers and with new writers and what would be called Good Books, "quality writing." I was so concerned with the writing of my own authors that I considered their books my own and I treated them as such. I entered into their creative process. Nevertheless, I was caught in the competitive crush and thrust of commercial publishing. There was no question of my own writing. I was relieved not to have to worry about my own writing. I scarcely grieved it, or mourned it. It had brought me so little—no more than itself.

I suddenly was not a man who I had known. I was on the phone . . . I hate phones, I really can't manage phones well. I won't answer it generally and if I do I can't talk very long; I just can't do it. But here I was having to live and negotiate on the phone. Editors live that way. With agents and all that. . . . Here I was doing this for the first two or three years. I was drawing up contracts and I never knew what a contract was; I didn't know what they were about.

But I began to fail after the fourth year. I got very disturbed for all kinds of reasons . . . publishing, that's a corrupt thing sometimes. I had my way for a while but then pretty soon night must fall and I was back with the old budgets and best-selling books and a lot of crap.

INTERVIEWER: I take it your interest in your own writing increased during those six years?

GOYEN: Yes, that was bound to happen. As years passed, I began to be hungry and I wasn't quite sure what that hunger was. Well, of course, it was that I was not writing, and the more I exhausted myself with other writers, the more hungry I became to do my own work. This is an exhausting thing, being an editor, and I had no time left for my own work, no matter how much I wanted it. The demands made on me were almost unbearable. And that was when I left McGraw-Hill—or was asked to do so by Albert Leventhal.

INTERVIEWER: That was in the '60s. In the '50s you were teaching at The New School. Did you find teaching just as demanding? Or was this a more satisfactory way to earn an income while doing your own writing?

GOYEN: Teaching writing is draining, too, of course. Especially the way I do it. You see, I believe that everybody can write. And in believing and teaching this, what happens, of course, is enormous productivity on the part of many students. One's students produce so much that he is followed down the street by the mass of stuff he's encouraged! I mean, he's overtaken by it. And there's that much more work to do and more conferences to hold, and it's a depleting and exhausting thing. Just as exhausting as editing.

INTERVIEWER: Is there an ideal occupation for the writer, then? Other than teaching?

GOYEN: Probably teaching is ideal. Because there's a community of writers there, and because the writer is respected and understood as a writer in colleges now. He's brought there as a writer, so it's understood why he's behaving the way he does and what he's doing when he's not around; he's *expected* to write. It's well-paid, now, too—universities are paying writers well. It's probably the best. It takes a lot of discipline for a writer to teach writing, though. But in the end, leading writing seminars and workshops is refreshing and exhilarating and creative and in touch with life. I consider teaching one of my callings.

INTERVIEWER: What do you think of your students?

GOYEN: The young people I've been involved with in my classes seem to have no sense of place. It bewildered me at first and then it caused me no little alarm. We've talked about it and what they tell me is often what I've presumed . . . that there isn't much of a place where they come from. I mean, every place looks like every other place. Even suburban places—around here or in Ohio or wherever—all look alike . . . a shopping center, a McDonalds, the bank with the frosted globes on the facade, you know, that's a given building. The repertory theaters all look alike. So that they really don't have a sense of place except through literature. But when they begin to write they can't write about Flaubert's place. So what they're writing about right now is the Princeton campus, and I've told them I don't want to hear about that. I ask them, but didn't you live somewhere before? Wasn't there a room somewhere, a house? A street? A tree? Can't you remember?

There was always a sense of belonging to a place in my childhood. The place. We called the house "the place." "Let's go back to the place," we'd say. I loved that. There was such a strong sense of family and generation and ancestors in it. It was like a monument . . . that's what my impression was and I wrote about it as that. It was a Parthenon to me . . . with that enduring monumentality to it. But these students . . . they've had terrible family problems—they are dissociated . . . they're so disoriented . . . divorce, my God, divorce is a way of life in these generations. I ask them, don't you have a grandmother? Do you ever go to your grandmother's? Where does she live? Oh, they say, she lives with us; or she lives in an apartment; she lives in the condominium. These elegant old ladies, they don't live in places anymore, either.

INTERVIEWER: To get back to your own work, do you feel that music is reflected in your writings?

GOYEN: It's an absolute, basic part of my work, there's no question, and I think of my writing as music, often; and of my stories as little songs.

INTERVIEWER: "Little songs," of course, is the literal meaning of the word "sonnet." The Albondocani Press has just published an edition of your early poems, poems written before your first novel. What made you abandon poetry for fiction? Faulkner said that all short story writers are failed poets. Do you feel this is so?

GOYEN: I think an awful lot of them are. I'm not a failed poet, I'm just a poet who made another choice, at a certain point, very early. Actually I'm so taken by the dramatic form I'm really a playwright manqué! I still consider myself, after having written and seen produced four plays in the professional theatre, manqué in the theatre. And yet I continue to love the form and fear it more than love it.

INTERVIEWER: Do you think your playwriting has been beneficial to. your fiction writing?

GOYEN: I think it has. I think it's made me care more about writing fiction, for one thing.

INTERVIEWER: Do you feel a compromise in the collaborations between director and producer and writer?

GOYEN: No, no, that's welcome to me, all that. I need all the help I can get! I never accept playwriting as a solitary thing. Once you do, you're ruined: because from the beginning it's a collaborative affair, and the sooner you can get it on to a stage, the better. The more you write at the table on a play, alone, the farther away you're going to get from the play. So far as the theatre is concerned, it becomes a *literary* work the more you work on it. But writing for the theatre has made me understand plot. It's helped me with plot in fiction writing.

INTERVIEWER: What European authors and what American authors have meant the most to you?

GOYEN: As for American authors, Hawthorne and Melville have meant a great deal. And Henry James. And two poets—Ezra Pound and T. S. Eliot—have influenced me.

INTERVIEWER: In what ways? They seem odd choices for a Southwestern fiction writer . . .

GOYEN: I still read, I still study, The *Cantos* of Pound. I found Pound in Texas when I was eighteen or nineteen through a young friend named William Hart. Hart was one of those prodigies, *enfants terribles*, that materialize in small towns, young men bearing a sense of art and poetry and life as naturally as others bore the instinct to compete and to copulate. He had a great deal to do with my early enlightenment and spiritual salvation in a lower middle class environment in an isolated (then) Texas town, where a boy's father considered him a sissy if he played the piano, as I've said, and questioned the sexual orientation of any youth who read poetry.

William Hart was a true pioneer; he brought me Pound, Eliot, and Auden. He was self-taught, finding things for himself out of hunger. He had a high-school education, barely, but afterwards he came and sat in my classes at Rice and listened. He knew more than the professors did some-times—he really did . . . about Elizabethan drama, and medieval ro-mances. He knew these things. He was a delicate boy, obviously, but not effete. He was French Cajun, from a poor family, and he was on the streets, and could have been in trouble a lot. But he ended up in the library. They felt they had a revolutionary in there. In the Houston Public Library at nineteen he would get up and speak about literature, and Archibald Mac-Leish, of all people. And oh, how this man Hart spoke. The whole library would turn and listen. He became that kind of town creature, one of those who go down in cities, unheralded . . . they go down into beds of ashes. Well, he brought me Pound.

Pound's *Cantos* hold for me madness and beauty, darkness and mystery, pain, heartbreak, nostalgia. Some of the most beautiful and most haunting were written as a prisoner. He made, above all, *songs*, and he told his stories lyrically, as I have felt driven to tell mine. By ordinary speech, ordinary people. I mean that it seems to me that Pound sometimes speaks from a sort of subtone in his poems like a con-man, a back-street hustler, using pieces of several languages, bits of myth, literary quotations and mixed dialects and plain beguiling nonsense. There is a stream, flowing and broken, of *voices* in Pound, echoes, town speech, songs, that deeply brought to me my own predicament, in the home of my parents and in the town where I lived. He helped show me a way to sing about it—it was, as most influences have been for me, as much a *tone*, a sound, a quality, as anything else.

The same for T. S. Eliot. He seemed then so much more American than Pound—but then Pound has the Chinese calligraphy and the heavy Greek and Latin. Eliot's wan songs broken suddenly by a crude word or a street phrase directly influenced me as a way to tell *The House of Breath*; and doom cut through by caprice shocked me and helped me survive in my own place until I could escape; showed me a way of managing the powerful life that I felt tearing through me, and trying to kill me. I saw a way: "Cry, what shall I cry?"—the dark biblical overtone of the great poem; "the voice of one calling Stetson!" Oh, Eliot got hold of me at that early age and helped me speak for my own place.

The storytelling method of Eliot and Pound—darting, elliptical, circular, repetitive, lyric, self-revealing, simple speech within grand cadence and hyperbole, educated me and showed me a way to be taken out of my place, away from my obsessing relations: saved me from locality, from "regionalism." I knew then that it was "style" that would save me. I saw Pound as the most elegant of poets and the most elemental. Both. His madness partakes of both (elegance and elementalness) and is a quality of his poetry: "Hast 'ou seen the rose in the steel dust / (or swansdown ever?) / so light is the urging, so ordered the dark / petals of iron / we who have passed over Lethe." That's Canto 74, from the *Pisan Cantos*.

INTERVIEWER: What of the Europeans?

GOYEN: Balzac above all, if just for the sheer fullness of story in him, for the life-giving detail in his novels. The daily *stuff* and the *fact* of his writing helped me struggle against a tendency toward the ornate and fantastical and abstract. Then come Flaubert, Proust. Of the English, Milton—a curious choice, right? The minor poems of Milton, but *Paradise Lost* above all. Milton's richness and grandness—his *scope*. I had an *epic* sense of my story, my material, and he helped me see it. Then Dante—the *Inferno*. Heine's poems—their sweet-sadness. The beautiful lyric poems of Goethe. Thomas Mann's stories, especially "Disorder and Early Sorrow," and *Budden-*

brooks. And some of the lyrical poems of Wordsworth. Poetry has been a strong influence on me, you see. I read it as often as fiction.

INTERVIEWER: You weren't influenced by Faulkner in any way?

GOYEN: No, not at all. His work is monumental, and extremely important to me, but not in any way an influence. It goes along beside me—*Light in August, Absalom, Absalom!*—but not through me. I can't say why, but I know that that's true. Maybe he's too *southern*. If that is a tradition . . . I'm not part of that. Thank God for my southwestern-ness . . . that Texan thing. My father, I'm afraid, is a southerner, a Mississippian, but my mother and her family for generations were native Texas people . . . so that was a strong influence. I knew a lot of my father's family; they're the people I've really written about in *The House of Breath*. But something kept me away from those sicknesses and terrors that come from that Deep South.

INTERVIEWER: *The House of Breath* came out at the same time as other celebrated works—Styron's, Capote's, Mailer's. Did you feel part of a writing generation?

GOYEN: I felt immensely apart. And most certainly did not belong to any "writing generation." I remember, indeed, saying, in an interview with Harvey Breit in 1950 in the *New York Times*, that I felt excited about joining the company of those writers, but that I had not before that time been aware of any of them! I stayed off to myself. I read nothing of "the literary world" when writing *The House of Breath*.

INTERVIEWER: Subsequently, did you ever do any reviews of your contemporaries?

GOYEN: I reviewed *Breakfast at Tiffany's* for the *New York Times Book Review*. Actually it was a fair review . . . but it was critical . . . I called Capote a valentine maker and said I thought he was the last of the valentine makers. Well, this just seemed to shake his life for the longest time.

INTERVIEWER: Do your contemporaries interest you now?

GOYEN: They really don't interest me very much. I still feel apart and, well, I *am* apart from my contemporaries. And they don't know what to *do* about me, or they ignore me. I am led to believe they ignore me.

INTERVIEWER: Hasn't that perhaps something to do with your books having been out of print for a decade or more, until recently?

GOYEN: No, I don't think so. How could it? My books have been in libraries, on reading lists in universities. Somebody was always writing a thesis or a paper on my work and writing to me for my help.

But: if I am so full of the books of all these people—Doris Lessing and

John Updike and X and Y and Z—how will I have a clear head for anything of my *own?* I'm really not very interested in contemporary fiction, anyway. I consider my fiction absolutely separate and apart from and unrelated to "contemporary American fiction."

INTERVIEWER: You feel closer to the European literary tradition?

GOYEN: I do.

INTERVIEWER: Your books continued to remain in print in European editions long after they were unavailable here. Do you have any notion why that is?

GOYEN: No, unless it was because my books were translated by such eminent translators—Ernst Robert Curtius and Elizabeth Schnack in Germany, Maurice Edgar Coindreau in France.

INTERVIEWER: All your novels have a rather unique form: they do not follow a linear line, for one thing. Did *The House of Breath* ever take form as a straightforward narrative and then later get broken down into monologues?

GOYEN: No, no, no. The form of that novel is the way it was written. It was slow, although it poured from me and a whole lot of it was simply *given* to me, absolutely put into my mouth. There were great stretches when nothing came. Then it poured out . . . in pieces, if that's possible. So, I thought of it as fragments . . . that was what established its form. I once called it *Cries Down a Well*, and then I called it *Six Elegies*. Later it was *Six American Portraits*. So it came in pieces, but I knew that they were linked.

INTERVIEWER: What do you have against the linear novel?

GOYEN: I always *intend* to write a linear novel when I begin. It's my greatest ambition to write a straightforward novel, and I always feel that I am, you know. I get very close. I thought *Come, the Restorer* was very close to being a linear novel. Then people laughed at me when I finished and said that's not true at all.

INTERVIEWER: What people?

GOYEN: Friends or interviewers, I suppose. What I end up writing each time, you see, is a kind of opera. It's a series of arias and the form is musical, despite myself, and it is lyrical. The outcry is lyrical despite myself. These novels have come to me at their height, passages have come to me in exaltation. So that the gaps between have been my problem and the—I was going to say—*quieter* . . . spaces and moments . . . but I don't mean that, because there are *many* quiet spaces in these books. But the less *intense* spaces seem to be hard for me to manage, somehow. What seems meant for me to do is always to begin what's called the linear novel, and try and try and try . . .

INTERVIEWER: Going back to form: Do you think of the novel as a lot of short stories, or as one big story? Or does it depend upon the novel?

GOYEN: It might. But it seems to me that the unified novel, the organic entity that we call a novel, is a series of parts. How could it not be? I generally make the parts the way you make those individual medallions that go into quilts. All separate and as perfect as I can make them, but knowing that my quilt becomes a whole when I have finished the parts. It is the *design* that's the hardest. Sometimes it takes me a long time to see, or discover, what the parts are to form or make.

INTERVIEWER: Does the completion of one "medallion" lead to another?

GOYEN: No, the completion of one medallion does not usually lead to another. They seem to generate, or materialize, out of themselves and are self-sufficient, not coupled to, or, often, even related to, any other piece. That seems to be what my writing job is: to discover this relationship of parts. Madness, of course, comes from not being able to discover any connection, any relationship at all! And the most disastrous thing that can happen is to *make up*, to *fake*, connections. In a beautiful quilt it looks like the medallions really grow out of one another, organic, the way petals and leaves grow. The problem, then, is to graft the living pieces to one another so that they finally become a living whole. That is the way I've had to work, whatever it means.

INTERVIEWER: Have you made medallions that did not fit into the final quilt?

GOYEN: There's rarely been anything left over, that is, medallions that didn't fit into the final quilt. If the pieces didn't all come together, the whole failed. It's really as though all the pieces were around, hidden, waiting to be discovered, and there were just enough for the design on hand. If, in rare cases, something was left over, one tried to use it as some sort of preamble or "postlude"—that sort of fussy thing. It never worked, even when one felt it was such "fine" writing that it should be kept in. It's this kind of exhibitionism of bad taste that's harmed some good work by good writers.

INTERVIEWER: So you started writing under a quilt and you came out producing quilts.

GOYEN: Producing them is right.

INTERVIEWER: How else would you describe your own writing, or your style?

GOYEN: As a king of singing. I don't say this because others have said it. But we've spoken of my work as song, earlier, the musicality of my writing and its form. It's impossible for me not to write that way. I write in cadence —that could be very bad. Just as in the theatre, when an actor in rehearsal discovers that lines in a speech rhyme, he or the director is horrified. Someone in the back of the theatre will scream out, "Couplet! Couplet!", meaning, "It rhymes! It rhymes!"

Now, when I speak of writing in cadence, I obviously don't mean "Couplet! Couplet!" Nor am I concerned with alliteration or any kind of fancy language. But I am concerned with the *flow* of language (the influence of Proust). I think of my writing as having to do with singing people: people singing of their lives, generally, arias. The song is the human experience that attracts me and moves me to write.

INTERVIEWER: Are you concentrating now on short stories or novels?

GOYEN: I have less an urge to write the short story, and more of a concern with writing The Book. It has nothing to do with anything but my own lack of a need for the very short form and a deep love for the book itself, for a longer piece of writing.

INTERVIEWER: Some may say you achieved both in *Ghost and Flesh*—a book of short stories which, on rereading, seems a total book rather than a collection of pieces. Was it conceived as a book, or was it a true gathering?

GOYEN: No, it was conceived as a book, it truly was. A sort of songcycle, really, that made up a single, unified work, a thematic unity like Schubert's *Die Winterreise* (which influenced *The House of Breath*—an early Marian Anderson recording. Frieda Lawrence first made it known to me, that is, the poem on which the songs were based).

Ghost and Flesh . . . you can see in those stories . . . wow . . . quite surreal and I loved those, and when that was finished and published, I kind of went off the beam. I think the book made me quite mad; writing it, the obsession of that book; but, on the other hand, *The House of Breath* did not. And that's an obsessed book, you see. It's hard to say these things but something always pulled me through. Of course my critics might say, he *should* have gone mad.

INTERVIEWER: What sort of madness was it:

GOYEN: While I wasn't that sane, I knew that madness—that's the word I use but I don't know if it's quite right—that dangerous thing . . . that terror, and I knew that. I guess I knew when to let it alone.

It comes in a loss of reality. If we say madness that sounds funny. But let's say an other-worldness. It has to do with identity. I go through phases of not knowing my own history. It's amnesiac almost. I've known this all my life; as a child I've known that. The loss of the sense of the world around me, of the reality. It means that I just have to isolate myself and then I'm OK.

Also, I found a very strong wife. So my choices must have been blessed. God knows, when I brought her home to Texas, people gathered to meet her and congratulate us and one woman came over to me who had known me all my life and said, "My God, I can't tell you how relieved we all are. We thought you were going to bring home some middle-aged *poetess!*"

INTERVIEWER: Is writing a work of nonfiction markedly different for you from writing fiction? Did you derive equal satisfaction from reconstructing the life of Jesus (in *A Book of Jesus*) as you do composing a novel?

GOYEN: Oh, yes. The excitement was tremendous in writing that book. There was no difference in feeling between that and what I felt when I had written fiction. It was as though I were creating a character in this man. A marvelous experience. Astonishing. A very real man began to live with me, of flesh and blood. He did the same work on me that He did on the people of the New Testament that He walked among: He won me over, enchanted and captured me, finally possessed me. I went rather crazy with the love from Him that I felt. I carried a little New Testament around with me in my pocket and would flip it open and read what He said, at cocktail parties or at dinner tables. A surprising reaction from my listeners generally followed: they were struck by the simplicity, wit, and beauty of what the man said to others, particularly to the wonderful woman at the well.

INTERVIEWER: How do you react to the charges of being a regional writer?

GOYEN: For me, environment is all. Place—as I was saying about my students—is absolutely essential. I know the vogue for the nonplace, the placeless place, á la Beckett, is very much an influence on writing these days. It has been said that places don't exist anymore. That everything looks alike. There is the same Howard Johnson on your turnpike in Kansas as there is in Miami and in the state of Washington. And the same kind of architecture dominates the new office buildings and the skyscraper. What is a writer to do? Free the "reality" of his environment? To lament loss of place, to search for it in memory? Because within place is culture, style. We speak of a lost way of life. In many of my books and stories, I've felt the need to recreate, to restore lost ways, lost places, lost styles of living.

INTERVIEWER: Isn't this what Marietta did in *In a Farther Country*? And what was expected of Mr. De Persia, in *Come, the Restorer*?

GOYEN: Exactly. So to this extent, then, I *am* a regional writer. In that my writing begins by being of a region, of a real place. It begins with real people talking like people from that place, and looking like them. Very often regional reality ends there and these people become other people, and this place becomes another place. The tiny town of Charity, in *The House of Breath*, is really Trinity, Texas, truly, accurately described. Once described, however, it ceases to be Charity or Trinity and becomes . . . well, London or Rome. The pasture in front of the house in Charity where a cow named Roma grazed becomes the Elysian Fields, and Orpheus and Eurydice flee across it. The house itself becomes a kind of Parthenon, with friezes of ancient kin.

I think there are moments when I exceed myself as a human being, and become Ulysses, perhaps, or Zeus. It is the point of time at which the human exceeds himself, is transformed beyond himself, that I most care about writing about. This is the lyrical, the apocalyptic, the visionary, the fantastic, the symbolic, the metaphorical, the transfiguratory, transfigurational—all those terms which have been applied to my work.

Now, by "exceeding myself as a human being" I mean in *life*—epiphany moments in life—not in *writing*. I mean those moments when human beings experience an epiphany, a transfiguration (that's the word) are the moments that most excite me. I've seen it in supreme artists who sang or danced or acted, in people who've told me they loved me, in those whose souls have suddenly been reborn before my eyes. These are moments and people I most care about writing about, no matter how small the moment, how humble the person. "I seen the little lamp," the transfigured child said at the end of the Katherine Mansfield story.

INTERVIEWER: Are your closest friends writers? Is talking to other writers helpful or harmful to your work?

GOYEN: My closest friends are theater people. Painters were once closest to me. For some years I lived among painters. But that changed. Now it's either performers or directors. I love theater people, they give me a great deal. I don't particularly like writers, and I am not prone to talk about writing. Since they're solitary workers, writers tend to *act out* in public, I believe. They seem to carry more hostility maybe because they are responsible to more people (their characters), to a whole world—like God—than painters or actors. Maybe it's because writers are caught in the English language, which sometimes seems like a sticky web you can't pull your antennae out of, like insects I've watched in webs, and are, in public and when they're with other people, still thrashing about in an invisible web. It is *enraging* to work in words, sometimes; no wonder writers are often nervous and crazy: paint seems to be a more benevolent, a more soothing and serene-making medium.

Musicians always want to play for you, which is wonderful and wordless; painters seem to want to talk only about sex or point out to you the hidden genital configurations in their canvas! Since the writer is truly a seminal person (he spits out his own web, as Yeats said, and then, as I just said, gets caught in it), the truly creative writer, I mean, he's full of the fear and the pride that a maker of *new* things feels. So it's seemed to me.

INTERVIEWER: After one of your books is done, do you divorce yourself from the characters, or do you seem somehow to maintain a contact with them?

GOYEN: Oh, the characters in my first novel haunt me to this day! Actually *haunt* me. And characters like Oil King (from *Come, the Restorer*) who's been in my life a long, long time. I've lived with him and loved him and written about him for many, many years. They stay with me, yes indeed they do. They stay. They not only enter my life but I begin to see them in life, here, there. I see Marietta McGee quite frequently, in several cities. I had not dreamt she was down in Enseñada, Mexico, until recently when I was there. They seem absolutely to exist in life, when I've seen some of them transferred to the stage: like Oil King in *The Diamond Rattler*—it's as though they read for the part and got it—read for their own role. And Swimma Starnes crops up a lot.

INTERVIEWER: How much of a plan do you have before you begin a novel or a play?

GOYEN: I plan quite a bit. But I'm not too aware of it. That is, I've not got it all down, but I've got a good deal of it thought through or *felt* through, before I begin writing. So that the whole world of it is very much alive and urgent for me. I'm surrounded by it—almost like a saturating scent. I feel it like a heat. The world that I'm going to write has already been created, somehow, in physical sensation before I go about writing it, shaping it, organizing it. My writing begins physically, in *flesh* ways. The writing process, for me, is the business of taking it *from* the flesh state into the spiritual, the letter, the Word.

INTERVIEWER: Do you see, from *The House of Breath* to your latest novel, a progression? Do you see any new directions forthcoming?

GOYEN: There *is* a progression. I'm much freer. And I see a liberation of certain obsessive concerns in my work, a liberation towards joy! I feel that I'm much freer to talk about certain aspects of human relationships than I once was. . . . What was the other question?

INTERVIEWER: Do you see any new directions in your subjects or forms?

GOYEN: That's very hard to say. I'd find that only as I write on. I *do* want very much to write a heavily plotted novel, a melodramatic novel.

INTERVIEWER: Finally, a last question: Why do you write?

GOYEN: And the easiest to answer! I can't imagine *not* writing. Writing simply is a way of life for me. The older I get, the more a way of life it is. At the beginning, it was totally a way of life excluding everything else. Now it's gathered to it marriage and children and other responsibilities. But still, it is simply a way of life before all other ways, a way to observe the world and to move through life, among human beings, and to record it all above all and to shape it, to give it sense, and to express something of myself in it. Writing is something I cannot imagine living without, nor scarcely would want to. Not to live daily as a writing person is inconceivable to me.

Notes and References

Chapter One

1. *The House of Breath* (New York, 1950), p. 11.
2. *The Faces of Blood Kindred* (New York, 1960), p. 52.
3. *The House of Breath*, p. 31.
4. *The Faces of Blood Kindred*, p. 75.
5. *The Collected Stories of William Goyen* (Garden City, 1975), p. 4.
6. *The House of Breath*, p. 18.
7. *The Faces of Blood Kindred*, p. 19.
8. *Selected Writings of William Goyen* (New York, 1974), p. 2.
9. "The Art of Fiction," *The Paris Review* (Winter 1976), pp. 60–61.
10. *Ibid.*
11. *Ibid.*
12. "Talk with William Goyen" by Harvey Breit, *New York Times Book Review*, Sept. 10, 1950, pp. 2.
13. Letter from William Goyen to Clyde Grimm, July 17, 1970.
14. *Ibid.*
15. *Ibid.*
16. *The House of Breath*, 25th Anniversary edition (New York, 1975).
17. *Selected Writings of William Goyen*, p. 2.
18. *Ghost and Flesh* (New York, 1952), p. 147.
19. *U.S.I.S. Feature*, Nov. 28, 1955, p. 84.
20. *Selected Writings of William Goyen*, p. 2.
21. Breit interview.
22. Preface, *Collected Stories of William Goyen*, p. 4.
23. Quoted on dust jacket of original edition (1950).
24. Quoted on dust jacket of *Ghost & Flesh* (1952)
25. Quoted on dust jacket (1950).
26. *Ibid.*
27. Quoted on dust jacket, second edition (1975).
28. "About the Author," dust jacket copy, *In a Farther Country* (New York, 1955).

29. Letter from William Goyen to Margaret L. Hartley, quoted in *Southwest Review* (Summer 1954); 284.

30. Letter from William Goyen to Robert Phillips, July 13, 1969.

31. Letter dated July 17, 1970.

32. *Ibid.*

33. *Ibid.*

34. Letter from William Goyen to Blanche Gregory, Oct. 19, 1971.

35. Letter from William Goyen to Robert Phillips, Aug. 16, 1971.

36. Letter from William Goyen to Robert Phillips, May 16, 1976.

37. "The Art of Fiction," *Paris Review* (Winter 1976), p. 100.

Chapter Two

1. *The Captain's Death Bed and Other Essays* (New York, 1950), pp. 58–59.

2. "About the Author," *In a Farther Country* (New York, 1955), p. 184.

3. *Granite and Rainbow* (New York, 1958), pp. 18–19.

4. *Pictures and Conversations* (New York, 1975), p. 171.

5. *The Novel of the Future* (New York, 1968), p. 44.

6. *Ibid.*, pp. 78, 115.

7. *Rediscoveries*, ed. David Madden (New York, 1971), pp. 256–62.

8. *San Antonio Express*, Aug. 27, 1950.

9. *Violence in Recent Southern Fiction* (Durham, N.C., 1965), p. 134.

10. *The Novel of the Future*, p. 115.

11. *The Poetics of Space* (Boston, 1969), p. 59.

12. *Essays on European Literature* (Princeton, 1973), p. 456.

13. *Surrealism in William Goyen*, p. 68.

14. *Houston Chronicle*, Aug. 20, 1950.

15. *The House of Breath*, p. 45.

16. *Ibid.*, p. 4.

17. *Essays on European Literature*, p. 461.

18. *Ibid.*, p. 462.

Chapter Three

1. *The American Short Story: Front Line in the National Defense of Literature* (Boston, 1964), pp. 122–23.

2. The term is Louise Y. Gossett's, used in her excellent chapter on Goyen, "The Voices of Distance," in her *Violence in Recent Southern Fiction* (Durham, N. C., 1965), pp. 131–45.

3. *The Art of Southern Fiction* (Carbondale, Ill., 1967), p. 129.

4. *The American Short Story*, p. 122.

5. *Violence in Recent Southern Fiction*, p. 136.

6. *Psychology and Religion: West and East, The Collected Works of C. G. Jung* (Princeton, 1969). XXI. 441.

7. *Ibid.*

8. *Ibid.*

9. *Ibid.*, p. 508.

10. *Ibid.*, p. 508.

11. *Ibid.*, p. 319.

Chapter Four

1. *The Art of the Southern Novel* (Carbondale, Ill., 1967), p. 127.

2. See Papus's *Traite methodique de science occulte* (Paris, 1891). Quoted in *A Dictionary of Symbols*, ed. J. E. Cirlot (New York, 1962).

3. See "The Editor's Notebook," *Southwest Review* 39 (Summer 1954): vi.

4. See the thirteenth-century *Zohar*, or "Cabalistic Bible," of Moses de Leon. Quoted in Cirlot (see note 2 above).

5. *Surrealism in William Goyen* (University of Bordeaux: unpublished dissertation, 1963).

Chapter Five

1. *The American Short Story: Front Line in the National Defense of Literature* (Boston, 1964), p. 123.

Chapter Six

1. The novel is titled *Savata, My Fair Sister* in the English edition and, for some reason, *Savannah* in the French.

2. Personal conversation with Robert Phillips, March 23, 1975.

3. *Violence in Recent Southern Fiction* (Durham, N. C., 1965), p. 143.

4. For this insight I am grateful to Yves Berger's Preface to *Savannah* (Paris, 1964), pp. 7–13.

5. "The Fair Sister," *Annual Essays-Reviews of 100 Outstanding Books Published in the United States During 1963*, ed. Frank H. Magill (New York, 1964), p. 77.

Chapter Seven

1. *In a Farther Country* (New York, 1955), p. 176.

2. *Come, the Restorer* (New York, 1974), pp. ix–x.

3. *Ibid.*, p. 59.

4. I am grateful to Patrice Repusseau's unpublished essay, "The Concentrated Writings of William Goyen: Reflections on *Come, the Restorer*," for first calling my attention to certain of these parallels.

5. *A Book of Jesus* (New York, 1973). Page references to this edition are in the text.

Chapter Eight

1. "William Goyen and His Work," *Book Forum*, 3, ii (1977), n.p.

2. *Come, the Restorer* (New York, 1974), p. 165.

3. "William Goyen and His Work," n.p.

4. "The Concentrated Writings of William Goyen: Reflections on *Come, the Restorer,*" unpublished essay by Patrice Repusseau, 1975.

5. *Ibid.*

6. *Ibid.*

7. *The House of Breath* (New York, 1950), p. 31.

Chapter Nine

1. Author's Note appended to *Nine Poems by William Goyen* (New York, 1976), p. 9.

2. *Nine Poems,* p. 15.

3. *William Goyen. Short Stories* (Göttingen, 1964), p. 3.

4. *The Collected Stories of William Goyen* (Garden City, 1975), p. 219. All references to the seven previously uncollected stories are to them as they appear in this edition.

5. Letter from William Goyen to Margaret L. Hartley, printed in *Southwest Review* 33 (Summer 1953): vi.

6. Review of *Collected Stories, Chicago Tribune Book World* (Nov. 9, 1975).

7. Louis K. MacKendrick, "Fiction Chronicle," *Ontario Review* 4 (Spring-Summer 1976): 101.

8. *Ibid.,* pp. 102–103.

9. Letter from William Goyen to Robert Phillips, Aug. 3, 1976.

10. I am grateful to Eva Taube for the suggestions of her "study questions" on this story, as printed in her anthology, *Alienated Man: Literature of Estrangement, Dissent, and Revolt* (New York, 1972), pp. 47–48.

Chapter Ten

1. *The Courage to Create* (New York, 1975), p. 8.

2. "Who is William Goyen?" *Sallyport* 30 (May–June 1975): 2–3. This and the following excerpts from Repusseau are from the same essay.

3. Review of *The Collected Stories of William Goyen, Globe Books* (Nov. 17, 1976), n.p.

Selected Bibliography

PRIMARY SOURCES

1. Novels

Come, the Restorer. Garden City: Doubleday, 1974.

The Fair Sister. Garden City: Doubleday, 1963. (As *Savata, My Fair Sister.* London: Peter Owen, 1963.)

The House of Breath. New York: Random House, 1950. (Reprinted, 25th Anniversary Edition, New York: Random House/Bookworks, 1975. Hardback and paperback.)

In a Farther Country. A Romance. New York: Random House, 1955. (Reprinted, London: Peter Owen Ltd., 1955.)

2. Story Collections

The Collected Stories of William Goyen. Garden City: Doubleday, 1975.

The Faces of Blood Kindred. A Novella & Ten Stories. New York: Random House, 1960.

Ghost and Flesh. Stories and Tales. New York: Random House, 1952.

Short Stories. Edited and Annotated by Erwin Helms. Göttingen: Vandenhoeck & Ruprecht, 1964.

3. Poetry

Nine Poems by William Goyen. New York: Albondocani Press, 1976.

4. Nonfiction

A Book of Jesus. Garden City: Doubleday, 1973. (Reprinted, New York: Signet Books, 1974)

My Antonia. A Critical Commentary. New York: American R.D.M. Corp., 1966.

Ralph Ellison's Invisible Man. A Critical Commentary. New York: American R.D.M. Corp., 1966.

5. Miscellany

Selected Writings of William Goyen. Illustrated by Elizabeth Fairbanks. New York: Random House/Bookworks, 1974. (Hardback and paperback.)

6. Translation

The Lazy Ones (Les Faneants) by Albert Cossery. New York: New Directions, 1949; London: Peter Owen, 1952.

7. Plays

A Possibility of Oil, produced on CBS television, Hollywood, 1958.

Aimee!, produced in Providence, Rhode Island, Trinity Square Rep. Theatre, 1973.

Christy, produced in New York, American Place Theatre, 1964.

The Diamond Rattler, produced in Boston, Charles Playhouse, 1960.

The House of Breath, produced in New York, Circle-in-the-Square Theatre, 1955.

The House of Breath, Black/White, produced in Providence, Rhode Island, Trinity Square Playhouse, 1969.

8. Song Lyrics

Score for the film *The Left-Handed Gun*, Warner Bros., 1956.

9. Uncollected Writings

"A Parable of Perez," *New Directions in Prose and Poetry*, No. 11 (New York: New Directions, 1949), 240.

"Precious Door," *Southwest Review*, Fall 1978.

"Right Here at Christmas," *Redbook*, December 1977.

"The Storm Doll," *Ontario Review*, Fall-Winter 1977–78.

"Three Poems," *Le Bayou* (University of Houston), 1941–42.

"While You Were Away," Houston Public Library, 1978.

10. Manuscript

"Half a Look of Cain," unpublished novel in William Goyen papers at Rice University.

SECONDARY SOURCES

1. Books and Parts of Books

BACHELARD, GASTON. *The Poetics of Space*. Boston: Beacon Press, 1964, pp. 58–59. Discusses Goyen's work in relation to memories and dreams and sees *The House of Breath* as a novel on the unreality of reality.

BLOTNER, JOSEPH L. "The Fair Sister," *Annual Essay–Reviews of 100 Out-*

standing Books. New York: Salem Press, 1964. An appreciative discussion of Goyen's third novel.

BRADBURY, JOHN M. *Renaissance in the South*. Chapel Hill: University of North Carolina Press, 1963, pp. 136, 196–97. Treats Goyen in relation to his generation of writers, mainly from the South rather than the Southwest, to which he rightfully belongs.

CURTIUS, ERNEST R. "William Goyen," *Essays on European Literature*. Princeton: Princeton University Press, 1973, pp. 456–64. Goyen's first novel explicated as a lyrical epic of alienation by his first translator; points out the laws of separation and reunion in his work.

DASHER, THOMAS E. "William Goyen." *Dictionary of Literary Biography*. Columbia, S. C.: Bruccoli-Clark, 1978. A biographical and bibliographical account.

EISINGER, CHESTER E. *Fiction of the Forties*. Chicago: University of Chicago Press, 1962, p. 243. Examines Goyen's evocation of place, use of stream-of-consciousness, and addiction to symbols in first novel.

GOSSETT, LOUISE Y. "The Voices of Distance: William Goyen," *Violence in Recent Southern Fiction*. Durham: Duke University Press, 1965, pp. 131–45. *The House of Breath* interpreted as a novel on the breaking apart of the world and one with a "multiple refraction" point-of-view.

HASSAN, IHAB. *Radical Innocence: The Contemporary American Novel*. Princeton: Princeton University Press, 1961, p. 103. Contrasts the supposedly "narrow" metaphoric range of Goyen's first novel with the novel of worldly affairs.

HELMS, ERWIN. "Introduction," *William Goyen. Short Stories*. Göttingen: Vandenhoeck & Ruprecht, 1964, pp. 3–4. Casts Goyen in the role of the outsider in a dollar-chasing world, longing to reestablish human feeling, a secure home, an intact world, and explores the idea of "kinship" in his fiction.

HOFFMAN, FREDERICK J. *The Art of Southern Fiction*. Carbondale, Ill.: Southern Illinois University Press, 1976, pp. 124–29. Examines philosophy and meanings behind Goyen's first novel and also, in one of the rare examinations, his second.

LUCAZEAU, MICHEL. *Surrealism in William Goyen*. Diplome d'Etudes Superieures, Universite de Bordeux, 1963. Presents Goyen's work as triumphs in "the first grade of Surrealism."

NIN, ANAIS. *The Novel of the Future*. New York: Macmillan Company, 1968, pp. 115, 166, 172, 182. Discusses Goyen's whole work as a synchronization of dream and human experience: "He is the poet of atmosphere, climate, mood, and subtle exchanges."

PEDEN, WILLIAM. *The American Short Story*. Boston: Houghton Mifflin
    Co., 1964 (revised edition, 1975), pp. 20, 122–23, 172. Discusses
    stories in both of the individual collections, especially in relation to the
    nature of reality in the world of Goyen's imagination.
PRESCOTT, ORVILLE. "The Young Decadents," *In My Opinion*. New York:
    Bobbs-Merrill, 1952, pp. 110–19. Considers Goyen, Buechner, and
    others as writers of "decadent" literature in the early 1950s.
REPUSSEAU, PATRICE. *An Approach to The House of Breath*. M.A. Thesis,
    Institut d'Anglais Charles V, Paris, 1974. The source of several critical
    pieces on Goyen published in this country that reveal Repusseau to be
    an astute critic.
RUBIN, JAMES D. *The Idea of an American Novel*. New York: Crowell,
    1961, p. 183. Contains brief treatment of *The House of Breath*.
SAROTTE, GEORGES–MICHEL. *Comme Un Frère, Comme Un Amant*. Paris:
    Flammarion, 1976. Places Goyen's work in a homosexual context and
    relates it to that of other American novelists from Herman Melville to
    James Baldwin. (Reprinted in English translation as *Like a Brother,
    Like a Lover*. New York: Anchor, 1978).
STERN, DANIEL. "On William Goyen's *The House of Breath*," *Redis-
    coveries*, ed. by David Madden. New York: Crown Publishers, 1971,
    pp. 256–69. A "Southern Gothic" interpretation, which sees the novel
    as one of doomed people against a doomed and shrinking landscape, a
    reading perhaps more appropriate for some of Faulkner's novels than
    for Goyen's.
STRAUMANN, HEINRICH. *American Literature in the Twentieth Century*.
    New York: Harper & Row, 1965, p. 128. Examines classical mythology
    and psychological realism in Updike, Goyen, others.
TAUBE, EVA. *Alienated Man: Literature of Estrangement, Dissent, and
    Revolt*. New York: Hayden Book Co., 1972, pp. 47–48. Contains nine
    study questions on Goyen's story "Figure Over the Town."

2. Articles, Essays, and Reviews

(Highly Selective: for a checklist of all reviews of Goyen's books, see that of
    Clyde Grimm, in *Bulletin of Bibliography*, 1977.)
ALLISON, ELIZABETH. "Vain Calling in the Twilight," *Arkansas Gazette*,
    Sept. 3, 1950. A review of the first novel, with emphasis on nostalgia.
ANON. *Kirkus* 18 (July 1, 1950); 363. Calls Goyen's first novel a display of
    "a special talent for the more selective reader."
———. *Publishers' Weekly*, Sept. 15, 1975, p. 46. On the human and
    artistic rewards of Goyen's *Collected Stories*.

————. *Kirkus* (Sept. 1, 1975): Homesickness as the basis for Goyen's writing, especially in the *Collected Stories*.

ASHFORD, GERALD. "William Goyen's First Book Fulfills High Expectations," *San Antonion Express*, Aug. 27, 1950, p. 10B. Favorable review of *The House of Breath*.

BARR, DONALD. *New York Times*, July 24, 1955, p. 17. Review of *In a Farther Country*.

BERGER, YVES. "La Nouvelle heroine de William Goyen i une negresse blonde," *Les Lettres Francaises*, April 8, 1964, p. 3. Discussion of *The Fair Sister* as translated into French.

CAPLAN, S. W. "The Fair Sister," *Albuquerque Tribune*, April 11, 1964. Sees Goyen's comic novel as a satire on the struggle between sin and pleasure.

CHEUSE, ALAN. "Revisiting the Prose of William Goyen," *Los Angeles Times*, June 30, 1974. Review of *The Selected Writings* which sees the author as possessing "all the apostrophic fervor of Thomas Wolfe but none of his defects."

CURTIUS, ERNEST R. "The First Work of a Young American," *Neue Schweize Schau*, March 1952; reprinted in *Essays in European Literature*.

DAVIS, ROBERT GORHAM. *New York Times Book Review*, September 29, 1963, p. 5. Overreaction to racial humor in *The Fair Sister* by an academic critic.

DERLETH, AUGUST. *Chicago Sunday Tribune*, March 9, 1952, p. 6. A science-fiction and fantasy writer looks at Goyen's ghost stories.

FRYE, NORTHROP. *Hudson Review* 3, iv (1950): 611. A review of *The House of Breath* by the author of *The Anatomy of Criticism*.

GARRIGUE, JEAN. *New Republic*, December 25, 1950, p. 20. A lyric poet's response to Goyen's lyric, poetic first novel.

GRAU, SHIRLEY ANN. *New York Times Book Review*, November 3, 1974, p. 73. Wrong-headed look at *Come, the Restorer*, totally missing the humor, together with high praise for Goyen's *Selected Writings*.

HICKS, GRANVILLE. "Literary Horizons," *Saturday Review* August 6, 1960, p. 14. Intelligent discussion of *Faces of Blood Kindred* by a critic who followed Goyen's career from the first.

HOBBY, DIANA. "A City Called Rose," *Houston Post*, Christmas Books issue, December 1974. An appreciation of the wild, bawdy humor and outrageousness of *Come, the Restorer:* "Inventing extravagant symbols, transposing fathers and sons, he projects these impossible characters against all the little shabbinesses of the real world."

KIRSCH, ROBERT. "A Feeling for Fireplaces," *Los Angeles Times*, May 10, 1976. Review of *Collected Stories:* ". . . his regionalism is a language, a vocabulary of characters, settings and events, a world which is identifiable but never merely parochial."

KRAMER, PETER G. *Newsweek*, November 11, 1974, p. 111. Review of *Come, the Restorer:* "Evoking this vanished world with brilliance and verve . . . he reminds us gently that there is no return, that in all probability nothing wondrous will happen—leaving us enriched but with a deep sense of loss."

LA FARGE, OLIVER. *Saturday Review of Literature*, September 9, 1950, p. 19. The Pulitzer Prize–winning novelist looks at Goyen's highly praised first novel.

LOWRY, ROBERT. *New York Times*, Feburary 10, 1952, p. 5. A review of *Ghost and Flesh*.

MORRIS, ROBERT K. *St. Louis Globe*, November 17, 1976. Review of *Collected Stories:* "Goyen, in short, is a rare artist: one able to marry form and content in such a way that truth becomes beauty and beauty truth."

MURRAY, MICHAEL. *Commonweal* 98 (July 13, 1973): 391. A brief but intelligent review of *a Book of Jesus*—perhaps Goyen's least-reviewed book.

OATES, JOYCE CAROL. "William Goyen's Life Rhythms," *New York Times Book Review*, November 16, 1975, p. 4. A highly appreciative review of Goyen's *Collected Stories* by one of America's outstanding story writers, who sees his stories as both meditations and poems.

PARONE, EDWARD. "What Kin Are We All?" *Hartford Courant*, August 27, 1950. A perceptive reading of *The House of Breath* at time of its publication.

PAUL, JAY S. "Marvelous Reciprocity: The Fiction of William Goyen," *Critique* (1977): 77–91. Analyzes the role of telling, loving, and healing in all of Goyen's major works.

PEDEN, WILLIAM. *Saturday Review*, March 22, 1952, p. 17. Praise for Goyen's first collection of stories by a critic who has made a specialty of the genre.

———. *New York Times Book Review*, August 7, 1960, p. 5. Review of *Faces of Blood Kindred*, substantially reprinted in his book *The American Short Story*.

PHILLIPS, ROBERT. "Samuels and Samson: Theme & Legend in 'The White Rooster,' " *Studies in Short Fiction* 6 (Spring 1969): 331–33. An examination of the role of mvth in Goyen's most famous short story.

———. "The Romance of Prophecy: Goyen's *In a Farther Country*," *Southwest Review* 56 (Summer 1971): 213–20. A look at ecology and exile in Goyen's neglected second novel.

———. "A Physical Jesus," *New York Times Book Review,* May 6, 1973, p. 3. A review of *A Book of Jesus* in relation to other biographies of Christ written by creative artists.

———. "Secret and Symbol: Entrances to Goyen's *House of Breath*," *Southwest Review* 59 (Summer 1974): 248–53. Two critical approaches to the difficult first novel, reprinted (with additions) in this present volume.

———. *Commonweal* 101 (November 1, 1974): 116–19. Praise for contents of *Selected Writings*, lament for the brevity, and a contrast of Goyen's stories with Grace Paley's.

———. "Goyen's Mythopeic Imagination," *Southern Review* (Spring 1979): Review of *Collected Stories* from Jungian perspective.

PICKREL. PAUL. *Yale Review* 40 (Autumn 1950): 192. Review of *The House of Breath.*

PORTER, KATHERINE ANNE. *New York Times,* August 20, 1950, p. 17. Says that first novel contains "the fullest, the richest, the most expressive" writing she has seen in some time.

REPUSSEAU, PATRICE. "Who *Is* William Goyen?" *Sallyport* 30 (May–June 1975): 2–3. Excellent biographical and critical overview by a French scholar, published by the Association of Rice University Alumni.

———. "In the Name of the Father, of the Son, and of the Oily Spirit," *Southwest Review* 60 (Winter 1975): 87–89. Perceptive review of *Come, the Restorer* emphasizing that novel's wild but controlled dives into fancy and dream.

RHODES, RICHARD. *Chicago Tribune Book World,* November 9, 1975. A review of the *Collected Stories*—more complete than most—which sees the author as one of our best writers, "a dealer in breath, whence come sighs, whispers, joys, lamentations, and, ultimately and most prosaically, life itself."

ROLO, CHARLES J. *Atlantic* 186 (September 1950): 81. Calls *House of Breath* "an ambitiously experimental book. . . . Coming as it does from a very young writer, it announces a notable talent which already has great verbal resources at its command."

STREIT, SAMUEL ALLEN. *Library Journal,* October 15, 1975, p. Review of *Collected Stories,* stressing the poetic quality of the body of work.

TINKLE, LON. "In Which We Hold Down the Whistle for Young Texan's Lyric First Novel," *Dallas Morning News,* August 20, 1950. Excellent early appreciation, with emphasis on Goyen's ear, diction, and epiphanies, by a critic who could be counted upon to see the worth in each of Goyen's successive publications.

———. "Virtuosic Feast from Bill Goyen," *Dallas Morning News*, November 24, 1974. Sees *Come, the Restorer* as an audacious attempt to explain the making of a modern metropolis—not in terms of economics or business or sociological adaptation to environment, but in terms of legend and poetic myth.

———. "William Goyen's Latest Novel Shows How Man's Dreams Condition Reality," *Dallas Morning News*, July 10, 1955. Calls *In a Farther Country* a "daringly experimental work, blending as it does the reality of dreams with the reality of dailiness, using mesmeric sorceries and invoking again, for adults, the childlike sense of wonder."

WARD, L. H. *Library Journal* 98 (April 15, 1973): 1296. Sees the relation of *A Book of Jesus* to "the furtiveness, frustration, terror and dead pursuit" of Goyen's earlier books.

WHITE, CHARLES E. "Texan Goyen Sounds New Cry in *House of Breath*," *Houston Chronicle*, August 20, 1950. Says that Goyen's "integrity is so great that he has destroyed our lingering 18th Century notions of what makes prose and what makes poetry."

ZETLIN, FLORENCE ANSKIN. "Extraordinary First Novel by Young Southern Writer," *Norfolk* (Va.) *Pilot*, August 27, 1950. Appreciative review of *The House of Breath*.

3. Interviews

ANON. "Portrait of the Artist as a Young Texan," *Sallyport* (Rice University) 32, v (June 1977): 6–8. A detailed biographical sketch followed by an interview conducted at the time Goyen received the 1977 Distinguished Alumnus Award from Rice.

BREIT, HARVEY. "Talk with William Goyen," *New York Times Book Review*, September 10, 1950, VII, 12. A sensitive piece sketching Goyen's character and his frame of mind immediately following the success of *The House of Breath*, with emphasis on the author's shyness and introspectiveness.

DUNCAN, ERIKA. "William Goyen and His Work," *Book Forum* 3, ii (1977): n.p. A subjective interview conducted by the young author of *A Wreath of Pale White Roses*.

GIUDICELLI, CHRISTIAN. "Je construis un monde a côte du monde," *La Quinzaine Litteraire* (November 1974). Concerns Goyen's search for harmony in nature and in the universe, particularly in relation to the writing of his first novel.

PHILLIPS, ROBERT. "The Art of Fiction, LXIII," *Paris Review* 68 Winter 1976): 58–100. Reprinted in its entirety as appendix to this book.

Index

DATE DUE